Teaching Religious Literacy

Offering resources and initiatives on religious and spiritual diversity in higher education, this book describes the conceptual foundations for teaching religious literacy and provides a sample curriculum with a facilitator's guide and assessment tools needed to evaluate its development among students. With a clear understanding of the diversity of religious and spiritual experiences found on college and university campuses, Ennis offers a much-needed framework for facilitating conversations about religion and spirituality in colleges and universities. By working from a comprehensive overview of NYU's award-winning Faith Zone training program, this book breaks down the methodology and tools required to create religious literacy training curricula at campuses around the world.

Ariel Ennis is Assistant Director and Senior Multifaith Educator at the Of Many Institute for Multifaith Leadership in the Office of Global Spiritual Life, and Adjunct Lecturer at the Silver School of Social Work at New York University, USA, and creator and host of the Multifaithful Podcast.

Teaching Religious Literacy

A Guide to Religious and Spiritual
Diversity in Higher Education

Ariel Ennis

Foreword by
Dr. Marcella Runell Hall

Routledge
Taylor & Francis Group

NEW YORK AND LONDON

First published 2017
by Routledge
605 Third Avenue, New York, NY 10017

and by Routledge
2 Park Square, Milton Park, Abingdon, Oxon, OX14 4RN

Routledge is an imprint of the Taylor & Francis Group, an informa business

Library of Congress Cataloguing-in-Publication Data
A catalog record has been requested

ISBN: 978-1-138-63585-2 (hbk)
ISBN: 978-1-315-20635-6 (ebk)

Typeset in Times New Roman
by Apex CoVantage, LLC

Contents

Foreword

> There was a time, not very long ago, when religion was all but invisible in the educational programming of most colleges and universities. That time is past; religion is no longer invisible.[1]

There are few things that get me more excited than talking, thinking, and reading about the intersection of spirituality and social justice, particularly in the context of higher education. So, when the opportunity to create a curriculum and training program to bring these topics to life presented itself, I absolutely knew I needed to go for it. My creative spark was ignited, and I began to share my idea for a "faith zone" with colleagues and students, and pretty much anyone else who would listen. This was nearly 5 years ago.

In the spring of 2012, I was given the opportunity of a lifetime: to co-lead a new program at New York University (NYU) called the Of Many Institute for Multifaith Leadership. The institute was being co-founded by Rabbi Yehuda Sarna, Imam Khalid Latif, Dr. Linda Mills, and Dr. Chelsea Clinton. I had spent the previous 5 years at NYU working on diversity education initiatives for the Center for Multicultural Education and Programs, and I was beyond thrilled to work with these tremendous colleagues in building a brand new institute, full of possibilities for social change, both at NYU and beyond.

One of my first goals was to rethink how diversity education related to religious literacy and multifaith dialogue. Condensing broad and complex concepts of religion in the context of diversity, education seemed untenable, and a place as "cosmopolitan" and diverse as NYU, which included over 12 global sites at the time, presents even more challenges. I began imagining the possibility of creating a "faith zone," a new way of thinking, teaching, and talking about religion and spirituality that was also paying homage to the phenomenal work of the LGBTQ "Safe Zone" programs. I imagined this introductory diversity education training as a place to begin finding shared language for talking about complex issues related to belief systems and religious tenets, experiences of identifying as atheist or agnostic, or even a "none," and learning to be comfortable having these conversations with classmates, colleagues, and other community members.

In preparing to develop the Faith Zone module, I recalled my early days at NYU when the only resource for religious life on campus was the nascent spiritual diversity network created by my colleague Stephen Polniaszek. Students loved it, and they demonstrated their interest in this area by continuously requesting the development of additional spiritual and religious groups. Yet, when we hosted major Diversity and Social Justice weekends programs, we usually left religion off the agenda and instead focused on race, class, ability, sexual orientation, and gender. At that moment in the late 1990s, a general sentiment in higher education seemed to be that it was too messy, complicated, personal, and perhaps even anti-intellectual to talk about religion and spirituality in the context of social justice and higher education.[2]

It wasn't until I left NYU in 2002 to begin my doctoral work in Social Justice Education at the University of Massachusetts (UMass), Amherst, that I started to truly connect the importance of religion to U.S. social movements, studying figures such as Martin Luther King Jr., Malcolm X, and Mother Theresa. As I strengthened my own understanding of pedagogy, curriculum, and using theory to create best practice, I began to develop concrete ideas about how to incorporate these critical elements into a more digestible model that could be used in a shorter-term context. But, it would be years before I was in the right place at the right time to take action.

After my time at UMass, before returning to NYU for a second time in 2007, I had the opportunity to be a fellow at the Tanenbaum Center for Interreligious Understanding, another experience that helped me create my first drafts of what would later become the seeds of Faith Zone. At NYU, I started piloting 90-minute conversations about religion with graduate students in the Future Administrators Cultural Training Institute at NYU, and later, as a 3-hour workshop in a different program I co-created at NYU, the Administrator Cultural Training Institute. I used data from the 5 years of running the ACT-I module to better hone the 3-hour short-term Faith Zone pedagogy. The formula remained consistent: goals, guidelines, name story, earliest memories of religious/spiritual significance (practicing multifaith dialogue), then terms, concepts, and statistics about why this is important in the world, the United States, higher education as a field, bringing it back to a local context (NYU), which culminated with a video or panel discussion of basic religious literacy provided by members of the (local) chaplain circle. I conducted no less than 30 pilot sessions of Faith Zone, including at NYU–Abu Dhabi, with the NYU Chaplains Circle, and general open sessions for students. I worked with interns, graduate students, chaplains, and staff members who helped perfect the early versions of the curriculum and believed so passionately in its potential and possibility.

The culminating piece for me came in creating a train-the-trainer module, which we could then use to educate and empower a whole new group of educators to be able to deliver the content throughout the NYU community and beyond. I am so proud of the direction and impact that Faith Zone has had: Other schools and organizations contacted us regularly to ask about the pedagogy, and well over 2,000 people have been trained to date. Furthermore, the Interfaith Youth Corp is in the final stages of developing a diversity education module called Bridges, in part inspired by the impact of a program like Faith Zone. The work of Interfaith Youth Corp, and Eboo Patel more specifically, is an incredible inspiration to the development of the original Faith Zone conversations, as Eboo's work is the perfect blend of activism, social change, dialogue, and service, in the context of religion and higher education.

The final stage, and an incredible train-the-trainer opportunity, came as I was preparing for maternity leave in the fall of 2013 and had accepted a new position at Mount Holyoke College. We had the tremendously good fortune of hiring Ariel Ennis to come on board to what was now the Global Spiritual Life Office, and he became the lead multifaith educator. Ariel has continued making changes and innovations in the curriculum, which you will read about in this book, while at the same time honing and enhancing key components related to religious literacy. He has also worked incredibly hard to create an innovative assessment rubric and sophisticated analysis of the impact of the work. With Ariel's work bringing Faith Zone to the next level, it was recognized in 2014 Inaugural Spiritualty and Religion in Higher Education Outstanding Spiritual Initiative Award from National Association of Student Personnel Administrators (NASPA).

Faith Zone has evolved into a cutting-edge diversity education program, which is proudly highlighted in the coming chapters. This important work will continue to impact and inspire many more students, faculty, and staff to become more comfortable with multifaith dialogue and more enthusiastic about becoming religiously literate. Our students deserve our very best about how to talk and think about our differences in a way that creates the communities we are capable of building. I believe in a future where our values, traditions, beliefs, differences, and commonalities are easily discussed and dissected, where we each get to be our whole selves, particularly in higher education.

> One of the dangers we face in our educational systems is the loss of a feeling of community, not just the loss of closeness among those with whom we work and with our students, but also the loss of a feeling

of connection and closeness with the world beyond the academy. Progressive education, education as the practice of freedom, enables us to confront feelings of loss and restore out sense of connection. It teaches us how to create a community.[3]

Marcella Runell Hall
Vice President for Student Life and Dean of Students
Mount Holyoke College, USA

Preface

Over the last few years, concerns about diversity and inclusion have become increasingly central to conversations about campus climates and the future of higher education in the United States. We have seen students at the University of Missouri, Yale, and campuses across the country demand campus-wide conversations about race, representation, and equity, contending that these conversations have long been neglected by their institutions. These conversations have been heated and controversial, bringing these issues to the forefront of campus conversations in the most focused way since perhaps the Civil Rights Era of the 1960s. Our students are demanding that institutions recommit themselves toward answering a central question: If higher education is designed to introduce young people to the ideas and philosophies needed to navigate the world, are we confident that the ideologies being represented in higher education are truly representative of the beliefs and identities present in our broader society?

As if an emotionally charged national conversation about race, representation, and equity were not challenging enough, diversity conversations within higher education are further complicated by the increasingly global dimension of educational institutions around the world. Nowhere is this more evident than at New York University (NYU), where our vision as a "Global Network University"[4] has increased the scope and complexity of our diversity conversations. Nearly 20 percent of NYU students are international students, and our increasing global presence has created portal campuses or study away sites in 13 countries on six different continents. This has brought new student populations to NYU, forcing our institution to introduce an entirely new dimension into an already complex topic. Therefore, if diversity and inclusion are increasingly important to the mission of higher education, and are simultaneously growing more complex, the approaches and tools that educational institutions bring to bear require more careful investigation than ever before.

Fortunately, there is reason to believe that, despite current imperfections, higher education is well equipped to respond to this challenge. Higher education has a long history of diversity initiatives that enable students, staff, and faculty to understand and embrace inclusion and equity in the face of difference. Across the United States, Safe Zone workshops to discuss issues of gender and sexuality are commonplace, and many institutions have additional programs that tackle other areas of diversity, including race, ethnicity, socio-economic class, and immigration status.[5] At NYU, this set of trainings is grouped together by a program called *NYU In the Zone* whose purpose is to enhance cross promotion of workshops and offer an ever-expanding skill set for working with complex issues of identity.[6] Within the National Association of Student Personnel Administrators, the largest student affairs professional association in the world, there are 10 listed focus areas, four of which are dedicated to diversity and the development of an orientation toward global citizenship.[7] And yet, despite this ubiquity of diversity education initiatives at universities across the country, there is one area that consistently lacks resources and curriculum development: religious and spiritual diversity.

Because of the constitutional separation of Church and State in the United States, educational institutions across the country have avoided conversations about religious and spiritual identity altogether, relegating these conversations to the privacy of dorm rooms rather than classrooms. The lack of resources available for religious and spiritual life is perfectly summed up by Eboo Patel, founder and President of the Interfaith Youth Core, who states:

> While higher education has stepped forward to do the hard—even heroic—work of engaging diversity issues related to race, gender, ethnicity, and sexuality, religious identity has too frequently been dismissed or treated with derision.[8]

To elucidate this dynamic, our office compiled a list of the top 100 universities in the 2015 U.S. News and World Report rankings (excluding religiously affiliated institutions) and compared the number of dedicated centers in each of the following three categories: LGBTQ, multicultural education, and spiritual life.[9] To simplify the data, the universities were ranked in each category on a scale of 0–2. A ranking of 0 indicates that the university has no dedicated center within a given category, or that it has purely academic or purely student-led initiatives addressing these issues (student clubs, academic departments, and institutes for religious studies). A ranking of 1 indicates that the university has (a) a division of student affairs without designated staff or a designated center, but which offers resources;

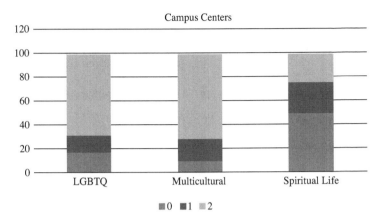

Figure 0.1 Diversity Centers at Top US Universities

or (b) a program within a particular school (example: Business School); or (c) a University Chaplain's office (for spiritual life); or (d) a diversity office (for multicultural) with limited staff/programming. A ranking of 2 indicates that the university has a designated director, dedicated staff, programming, and resources that are available to the entire campus. The findings indicate that while both LGBTQ and multicultural centers have similar numbers of dedicated programs at top universities (69% and 71%, respectively), spiritual life centers have less than a third the number of dedicated centers (23%). In addition, almost half of top universities (49%) do not have any dedicated resources for spiritual life (ranking of 0) as compared to only 17 percent for LGBTQ and 9 percent for multicultural centers.[10]

This resource allocation, however, severely underestimates the importance of religious and spiritual identity in the lives of college students. The need for further resources dedicated to this area of student life is most convincingly articulated by Astin, Astin, and Lindholm in their 2011 book *Cultivating the Spirit: How College Can Enhance Students' Inner Lives*. This book, based on a 7-year longitudinal study of a nationally representative group of American college students, provides two essential insights into our students' level of engagement with religious and spiritual needs. First, college students display an overwhelming interest in topics that relate to religious and spiritual identity when they enter college. For example, more than 80 percent of incoming freshman attended religious services in the year prior to enrolling (44% frequently) and 69 percent prayed regularly.[11] Additionally, at least two-thirds of incoming freshman endorse the following statements about religious and spiritual identity:

- I gain spiritual strength by trusting in a higher power.
- I find religion to be personally helpful.
- My spiritual/religious beliefs provide me with strength and guidance.
- My spiritual/religious beliefs have helped me to develop my identity.[12]

Moreover, this interest does not end once students reach college. The second critical finding of this book is that college students display a consistent interest in these questions throughout their time in college. For each of these four statements, the level of agreement from students remained essentially unchanged when questioned again during their junior year, "suggesting that students' level of religious commitment changes very little in college."[13] These shockingly high numbers imply that American college students are far more religiously and spiritually committed than people expect. Coupled with the lack of resources dedicated nationally to this facet of identity, we are faced with a higher education system whose students care deeply about religious and spiritual issues, but an institutional structure ill-equipped to meet these needs.

How do we begin providing resources to help students, staff, and faculty be more responsive to matters of religious and spiritual concern? To respond to this need, NYU created the Office of Global Spiritual Life (GSL) in 2012. This office is the hub for all religious and spiritual life at NYU and has three components. First, GSL provides administrative support for all religious and spiritual student groups at NYU. This includes finding space for religious services, providing guidance to religious student groups, and coordinating NYU's Chaplains' Circle, a group of over 60 chaplains from more than 20 different traditions and denominations who advise student groups and provide religious guidance for members of our campus. Second, GSL is home to MindfulNYU, which offers free daily yoga and meditation classes to students, staff, and faculty at NYU, as well as mindfulness programming collaborations with numerous NYU departments, including the Stern School of Business and the Silver School of Social Work. Third, and most important for this book, is the Of Many Institute for Multifaith Leadership. This component of our office has a simple mission: "to educate and inspire religious and spiritual leaders to utilize multifaith dialogue and service as a force for positive social change."[14] It is within this description for the Of Many Institute for Multifaith Leadership that we find the impetus behind this book. Once an institution has created a center to work with diverse expressions of religious and spiritual identity, the next logical question that must be addressed is how to facilitate educational conversations about these differences. What content should we teach people to prepare them for a cross-cultural experience? How should this content be delivered? How do we measure impact to prove whether or not our work has actually accomplished our goals?

At NYU, our solution to facilitating these conversations about religious and spiritual identity is Faith Zone. This curriculum creates a framework for facilitating conversations about religious and spiritual diversity on college campuses and beyond. Faith Zone provides a curricular framework that addresses many questions fundamental to discussing religious and spiritual diversity. This program has existed at NYU since 2012, and it is one of the few university sponsored programs in the world that directly addresses the challenges of discussing religious and spiritual identity in diverse environments. Faith Zone has become a nationally recognized curriculum, winning the 2014 Inaugural Spirituality and Religion in Higher Education Outstanding Spiritual Initiative Award. Faith Zone has also begun to spread beyond NYU's New York City campus, already having been taught at NYU–Abu Dhabi, NYU–Berlin, NYU–London, NYU–DC, and NYU–Washington Square, as well as at Utah State University, Mount Holyoke College, and the Pennsylvania Consortium of the Liberal Arts. As the staff person at NYU who runs the Faith Zone Program, I receive numerous calls each week from student affairs professionals at other universities asking how to create similar programs at their schools. This book will hopefully serve as a guide toward that goal, as well as provide tools and resources to enable other campuses to create similar programs that fit their unique campus cultures.

Terminology

Before laying out the structure for this book, it is important to take note of the various terms used by authors and researchers when discussing the religious and spiritual identities of students. A quick scan of the relevant literature reveals a plethora of seemingly interchangeable words including: religion, spirituality, faith, meaning making, and inner life. For example, the aforementioned *Cultivating the Spirit* advocates for the use of the term "spiritual development" and defends this choice as follows:

> Spirituality points to our inner, subjective life, as contrasted with the objective domain of observable behavior and material objects that we can point to and measure directly. Spirituality also involves our affective experiences at least as much as it does our reasoning or logic. More specifically, spirituality has to do with the values that we hold most dear, our sense of who we are and where we come from, our beliefs

about why we are here—the meaning and purpose that we see in our work and our life—and our sense of connectedness to one another and to the world around us.[15]

In contrast, Robert Nash, in his book *Religious Pluralism in the Academy*, prefers to utilize the term "meaning making." In his introduction, he states:

> I will attempt to construct a convincing rationale for administrators and faculty to address the needs of all students, both secular and religious, to make meaning. This is a meaning that incorporates, among other elements, a sense of transcendence, immanence and mystery; an enlargement of the moral imagination; and a genuine respect for religious and spiritual pluralism. I will be concerned mainly with religious and spiritual meaning, because this is the crux of the new faith revival both in larger society, and on college campuses everywhere.[16]

In these examples, we see authors using phrases such as "spiritualty," "values," "beliefs," "religious and spiritual meaning," and "purpose," all in reference to the same set of student concerns. This book, however, is not meant to determine a singular and perfect phraseology for this incredibly complex topic. In fact, the Faith Zone workshop utilizes these varied terms as a platform for exploring the complexities of religious and spiritual diversity. In the interest of simplicity, this book will refer to this broad spectrum of concerns under the heading "religious and spiritual," following the convention of the NASPA Spirituality and Religion in Higher Education Knowledge Community.[17] These terms are imperfect, but they provide a broad enough scope for this book, while simultaneously acknowledging the immense complexity and the plethora of alternate terms that would also be appropriate.

Outline of the Book

In the Preface of this book, I have argued that conversations about religious and spiritual diversity are central to the project of global higher education. Subsequent chapters will delve into the specifics of how we facilitate conversations about religious and spiritual diversity and elucidate the approach we have developed at NYU to address this topic.

Chapter 1 presents a conceptual analysis of the various approaches being used to facilitate cross-cultural religious and spiritual experiences in different contexts across the world. This analysis will focus on the various goals and intended outcomes that are articulated by these different initiatives, and how different approaches yield fundamentally different programs. This will create an essential foundation for understanding the goals of our particular approach, the "religious literacy" approach, and offer other approaches to supplement ours for sustainable long-term impact.

Chapter 2 analyzes the term religious literacy and expounds a framework for determining what content should actually be taught in religious and spiritual diversity workshops. Various scholars present vastly different definitions and articulations of this concept, and our analysis will serve as a foundation for understanding the definition and approach to religious literacy that we have chosen to use at NYU, as well as for all of the assessment materials against which we measure our success.

Chapter 3 presents the tools and materials we use at NYU for measuring the ongoing development of religious literacy among our students. These tools are fundamental to how we approach teaching Faith Zone, and articulate various stages of development that can be examined and measured throughout a student's experience on campus.

Chapter 4 presents the materials and structure that we use to translate the conceptual discussion of the first four chapters into a 3-hour workshop. We will share the assessment materials we use at NYU as well as present the five components of all Faith Zone sessions (setting the room, personal narrative, unpacking religious literacy, community snapshot, and takeaways and next steps). These components should be replicable in almost any context, and makes Faith Zone easy to reproduce and adjust in each particular campus and community.

In Chapter 5, we will share our curriculum for teaching religious literacy. This section contains sample slides and a facilitator's guide. For this curriculum, we owe a tremendous debt of gratitude to Dr. Marcella Runell Hall, Vice President of Student Life and Dean of Students at Mount Holyoke College, and co-founder and current advisory board member of the Office of Global Spiritual Life at NYU. She created the first religious literacy curriculum used at NYU and her insight can be found throughout the curriculum we use today.

In Chapter 6, we will look at measurable educational outcomes and begin to articulate the effect that a religious literacy training program can have on a campus. These data are culled from our pre- and post-session evaluations from the last 2 years, and they utilize our religious literacy rubric to evaluate participant learning in our sessions. These results should present a comprehensive explanation of the measurable outcomes we have witnessed from our religious literacy curriculum, as well as present some insight as to the best ways to approach the implementation of similar programs on other campuses.

Finally, in Chapter 7, we will discuss the applicability of Faith Zone to different types of campuses (public vs. private, religious vs. secular) and analyze various challenges we have encountered at NYU when teaching this material. This will involve challenges that are specific to being a large, secular private institution in New York City, as well as challenges involving specific student groups that have arisen since the foundation of our center. Finally, we will conclude with a few ideas about how to translate this work onto campuses across the country. We hope these materials are useful and insightful and that this book will contribute to an ever-growing field of study and inquiry surrounding religious diversity in higher education.

Notes

1 Douglas G. Jacobsen, and Rhonda Hustedt Jacobsen, *No Longer Invisible: Religion in University Education* (Oxford: Oxford University Press, 2012), vii.
2 Jacobsen and Jacobsen, *No Longer Invisible*, 23.
3 bell hooks, *Teaching Community: A Pedagogy of Hope* (New York: Routledge, 2003), xv.
4 Elizabeth Redden, "Global Ambitions," *Inside Higher Education*, March 11, 2013, accessed November 1, 2016, https://www.insidehighered.com/news/2013/03/11/nyu-establishes-campuses-and-sites-around-globe.
5 See Figure 0.1 and slide 24 in the sample PowerPoint.
6 Full List on slide 23 in the sample PowerPoint.
7 "NASPA Focus Areas," *NASPA—Student Affairs Administrators in Higher Education*, https://www.naspa.org/focus-areas.
8 Eboo Patel, "In Promoting Campus Diversity, Don't Dismiss Religion," *The Chronicle of Higher Education*, March 11, 2015, http://chronicle.com/article/In-Promoting-Campus-Diversity/228427/.
9 "The Best Colleges in America, Ranked," *U.S. News and World Report 20015*, http://colleges.usnews.rankingsandreviews.com/best-colleges.
10 See Appendix A. Credit to Hannah Leffingwell and Megan Montgomery.
11 Alexander W. Astin, Helen S. Astin, and Jennifer A. Lindholm, *Cultivating the Spirit: How College Can Enhance Students' Inner Lives* (San Francisco: Jossey-Bass, 2011), 83.
12 Ibid, 84–85.
13 Ibid, 85.
14 "Of Many Institute," *New York University*, accessed November 1, 2016, https://www.nyu.edu/students/communities-and-groups/student-diversity/spiritual-life/of-many-institute-for-multifaith-leadership.html.
15 Astin, Astin, and Lindholm, *Cultivating the Spirit*, 4.
16 Robert J. Nash, *Religious Pluralism in the Academy: Opening the Dialogue* (New York: P. Land, 2001), 14.
17 "Spirituality and Religion in Higher Education," *NASPA*, accessed March 30, 2016, https://www.naspa.org/constituent-groups/kcs/spirituality-and-religion-in-higher-education.

Acknowledgments

Our team at the Office of Global Spiritual Life is quite small, and every project relies heavily on student workers, chaplains, and partners to be successful. Faith Zone is no exception, and I want to thank everyone who got involved with Faith Zone over the last few years and helped make it such an essential program at NYU. Thank you to Avi Rothfeld, whose brilliance and hard work can be found throughout the curriculum. I also want to give special recognition to Hannah Leffingwell and Danit Fleishman, who played an instrumental role in editing and researching the book, and without whom, this book would never have gotten finished.

Thank you to the entire group of students and chaplains who worked with Dr. Marcella Runell Hall to create the original Faith Zone curriculum, including Arti Aryal, Alexa Friedman, Matt Hoffman, Grace Patterson, and Jessica Sears, the entire group of students in the Fall 2013 course "Whose Social Justice is it Anyway," and Chaplains Rev Mary Cat Young, Father John McGuire, and Rev Susan Field.

Thank you to Dr. Linda Mills for being the guiding light to our center and for her continued support for everything we do. Nothing in our office would be possible without her.

Thank you to Marc Wais, Senior Vice President of Student Affairs at NYU, for his leadership and consistent support of our office.

Thank you to Dr. Sonia Deluca Fernandez for her help with all assessment materials and being a sounding board as we tinkered with Faith Zone throughout the past few years.

Thank you to Yael Shy for being an incredible boss, mentor and friend. Her leadership is what makes our office run.

Thank you to Dr. Chelsea Clinton, Imam Khalid Latif, and Rabbi Yehdua Sarna for co-creating our center at NYU and for their collective leadership, guidance and support.

Lastly, thanks to my wife Rachel for being my best friend and a loving partner in everything I do, this book included.

1 A Priest and a Rabbi Walk Into a Bar

Now What?

There is no joke that more perfectly encapsulates the initial awkwardness of two people of different religions coming together than the plethora of jokes that begin with a rabbi and a priest walking into a bar (or an imam or monk walking into a coffee shop, if you are particularly savvy about religious diversity) with a clever mishap soon to follow. This joke holds a special poignancy in our world today as interfaith councils and activities have become increasingly commonplace in the wake of the World War II, and more recently, in the wake of the September 11th attacks. What is often unexplored, however, is the goal in bringing these people of different identities together in the first place. Therefore, before we fully explore *how* to engineer conversations about religious and spiritual diversity, it is first important to provide a quick scan of the world of multifaith engagement and a snapshot of the different approaches that are used by various organizations to create multifaith encounters around the word. These five approaches all intend to bring people of diverse religious and spiritual identities together, but to do so in distinct ways and with very different intended outcomes.

Community Building Approach

The approach to multifaith engagement that has the most concrete and specific foundation is what I term the community approach. This approach backs into a multifaith conversation by saying "we share this neighborhood or environment, and rather than hate each other, we should get along." This kind of shared community creates the foundation for many local interfaith councils or clubs on college campuses, and it may be the most common approach to this work. The ubiquity of these local interfaith councils is best highlighted by the research done by the Pluralism Project at Harvard University. This program, founded by Dr. Dianna Eck, one of the most important scholars of American religious diversity, has created a *Directory of Interfaith Organizations* from 20 major American cities.[1] This list is ever expanding and shows how common local interfaith councils have become in cities as different as Boston and Wichita. These groups often ignore difficult geopolitical conflicts such as Palestine–Israel, and instead focus exclusively on issues of local concern such as instances of intolerance in local communities. In essence, this approach is practiced as a foundational component to neighborly community building and should be a necessary component of any multifaith collaboration. We should always ensure that our religious communities make good neighbors.

Despite the obvious foundational importance of this approach, it is nevertheless important to highlight its most significant limitation. By focusing heavily on local communities, community-based groups are often ill-equipped to address the impact of global geopolitical events on community members. For example, during the escalation of violence between Israel and Hamas in the summer of 2014, I witnessed tension amongst members of our NYU community who were unsure of how this issue would influence their local friendships. Unfortunately, these groups are often left without the tools to properly address broader issues and concerns, leaving community members frustrated and confused when tensions arise around the world.

Exploring Spiritual Journeys Approach

Another common approach to interfaith work, and a derivative of the community approach, is to focus on shared spiritual experiences in an effort to build community by highlighting similar existential questions and desires. These events can often include shared text study, attending each other's religious services, or any other form of religious exchange that allows for people to explore the faith experience of someone else. This approach relies on an assumption that religious experiences across religions are fundamentally similar and that the exploration of these similarities can lead to relationship building and understanding.

The challenge to this approach is its accessibility for people whose religious traditions involve fewer rituals and holidays (such as Humanism) or people who have chosen to inhabit the less ritually observant end of the religious spectrum. For people who do not participate in prayer or other highly ritualized activities, this approach can prove inaccessible and fail to provide any foundation for further relationships. Moreover, this approach does not articulate any concrete actions or changes that should result from this work. Once people have attended these events and developed a higher degree of understanding, what are their next steps? How do they utilize this relationship to solve global problems? What is the long-term goal?

Service Approach

Perhaps the most popular approach to multifaith work among young people is what I term the service approach, exemplified by groups such as the Interfaith Youth Core (IFYC) and interfaith service trips undertaken by college students throughout the country during academic breaks. This approach focuses on areas of shared value and connection, and service to the community as the foundation for relationships that can transcend religious boundaries. This is one of the most common approaches and has been demonstrated to be effective in building relationships across religious divides. On NYU's Multifaithful Podcast, Eboo Patel, Founder and President of IFYC, frames this type of encounter as a fundamental component of being a citizen within a democracy.[2] Patel explains that diversity of expression and beliefs are critical to any democratic system, and the ability to navigate this difference is an essential skill that should be addressed in educational settings. He states:

> One of the most important things that interfaith groups can advance is the notion that people who orient around religion differently are going to disagree on fundamental things. They are going to disagree on matters of creation and salvation. They will likely disagree on matters of abortion and same sex marriage and where to draw the line in the Middle East. The question is, does disagreeing on some fundamental things entirely negate the possibility of working together on other fundamental things? I believe the answer to that has to be no in a diverse democracy.[3]

While I think that this formulation presents a compelling vision for bridging religious differences, our central question is not just how to bring people together who disagree on fundamental issues, but also how a sustained approach toward bridging religious divides can transform the world and solve global problems. This approach does not address two critical elements: How do we construct tools that enable deep dialogue around complex issues, and to do once this experience has concluded and participants return to their home communities? How do two people, once overtaken by goodwill from a service trip, create a substantial and sustained program that can tackle issues of conflict and controversy in the long term?

Peacebuilding in the Face of Conflict Approach

Until now, we have focused primarily on approaches that build relationships between people in regions or areas where there is relatively little conflict, but where there are at least two communities that have yet to seriously engage with one another. On the other end of the spectrum, there are organizations such as Seeds of Peace and PeacePlayers International that operate specifically with people who live in conflict zones and use peacebuilding strategies to directly reduce conflict. Seeds of Peace brings children from conflict zones to a summer camp in Maine to build relationships and break down barriers. They hope that in the long term, these students will become future leaders and transform the world. PeacePlayers International shares a similar long-term goal, but they accomplish it by focusing on sports and team building rather than facilitated interfaith dialogue. Both of these organizations tell stories of success and transformation (both websites are replete with awards and testimonials from luminaries such as UN Ambassador Susan Rice[4] and President Bill Clinton[5]), but it is difficult to measure the outcomes given the time lapse between a program working with teenage participants and their possible ascendance to a leadership role much later in life. Moreover, this model is fantastic for people from areas of conflict, but in areas without such a specific conflict, it is unclear whether such an approach has the necessary focus on religious and spiritual dialogue to truly facilitate powerful interactions. If there is no conflict at stake, what distinguishes an approach like this from any game of basketball on a regular playground in the United States?

Ethical Spectacle Approach

Most of the approaches we have focused on thus far avoid politics in favor of alternative means of bringing people together. There are many organizations, however, whose focus is actually the reverse: to bring like-minded political people of religious persuasion together for a political cause. This type of political action is described by the Auburn Seminary as an "ethical spectacle" and often generates the most publicity of any of these approaches. While this approach does not necessarily facilitate long-term relationship building and sustained engagement, it is hugely important for influencing media narratives about religious communities. For example, The Auburn Seminary built an arc to march in the People's Climate March in NYC to summon a religiously poignant image that could convey the importance of environmentalism.[6] This approach obviously did not create a sustained dialogue to bring people together, but rather focused on advancing a particular political narrative that could contribute to the larger environmentalist cause. This tool is especially effective when working on big-picture political issues, but lacks the ability on its own to facilitate long-term relationships and understanding among people who fundamentally disagree about life's biggest questions.

Taken together, these different approaches raise various questions about the central focus of multifaith work. Do we focus on shared experiences or our most bitter differences? Do we focus on global geopolitics or local issues? Do we engage in politics or remain apolitical? Do we act or study? Essentially, What is the goal of a multifaith collaboration?

Religious Literacy Approach

The final methodology I would like to introduce is the religious literacy approach. This approach puts the questions of shared experiences to the side and asks a more fundamental question: Can we teach people to have more productive conversations about religion and spirituality in diverse settings, and if so, how do we do it? This approach should work in tandem with the approaches listed above and should be a fundamental piece of any multifaith effort. Beyond simply providing programs and services, we should be asking deep questions about the content that we are conveying and the long-term outcomes we want to accomplish. This approach prepares the rabbi and the imam before they ever walk into the room, and it supports the articulation of a long-term vision of action and engagement that can solve our most challenging global issues.

Notes

1 "Directory of Religious Centers," *President and Fellows of Harvard College and Diana Eck*, http://www.pluralism.org/interfaith/directory.
2 Eboo Patel, "Eboo Patel on the Future of Multifaith," *Multifaithful Podcast*, December 2, 2015.
3 Ibid.
4 "PeacePlayers International," *Peace Players International*, accessed March 30, 2016, https://www.peaceplayersintl.org/.
5 "Our Advisory Board and Board of Directors," *Seeds of Peace*, accessed March 30, 2016, http://www.seedsofpeace.org/board/.
6 Isaac Luria, "Why We're Building an Ark," *Sojourners*, May 6, 2015, https://sojo.net/articles/why-we-re-building-ark.

2 Introducing Religious Literacy

If our goal is to teach people to successfully navigate conversations about religious and spiritual diversity by enhancing religious literacy, the question then becomes: How do we define, measure, and teach religious literacy? The most well-known articulation of religious literacy belongs to Stephen Prothero, author of the book *Religious Literacy: What Every American Needs to Know*. Prothero explains that religious literacy is "the ability to understand and use in one's day-to-day life the basic building blocks of religious traditions—their key terms, symbols, doctrines, practices, sayings, characters, metaphors, and narratives."[1] According to Prothero, as we become increasingly interconnected, the knowledge requirements for religious literacy are constantly expanding. As a guide to fostering this literacy, Prothero's book dives into fundamental areas of religious knowledge that can buttress religious literacy. His book lists over one hundred facts and definitions that are essential to becoming religiously literate, compiled together in a *Dictionary of Religious Literacy*,[2] as well as a sample religious literacy quiz at the end to test this knowledge. The strength of Prothero's formulation of religious literacy is his focus on discrete and knowable pieces of information that can be studied and understood. For Prothero, this approach to developing religious literacy is clear and accessible to anyone willing to read and study the relevant information. However, the weakness in this approach is that having knowledge of every single religious holiday, holy book, and ritual object does not guarantee that you have the tools and skills to approach someone who identifies in a different way and truly understand the depth and complexity of that person's identity. Discrete knowledge is of course helpful, but it is far too narrow for effectively navigating situations that involve the dynamic intersection of numerous religious identities at a given moment. Knowing details about religious theology alone does not make one more ready to engage with someone of a religious background you have never encountered before.

A second well-known approach to defining religious literacy has been formulated by Dianne Moore of the Religious Literacy Project at Harvard

Divinity School, and has been adopted by the American Academy of Religion. She states:

> Religious literacy entails the ability to discern and analyze the fundamental intersections of religion and social, political, cultural life through multiple lenses. Specifically, a religiously literate person will possess 1) a basic understanding of the history, central texts (where applicable), beliefs, practices and contemporary manifestations of several of the world's religious traditions as they arose out of and continue to be shaped by particular social, historical and cultural contexts; and 2) the ability to discern and explore the religious dimensions of political, social and cultural expressions across time and place. Critical to this definition is the importance of understanding religions and religious influences in context and as inextricably woven into all dimensions of human experience. Such an understanding highlights the inadequacy of understanding religions through common means such as learning about ritual practices or exploring "what scriptures say" about topics or questions. Unfortunately, these are some of the most common approaches to learning about religion and lead to simplistic and inaccurate representations of the roles religions play in human agency and understanding.[3]

This definition is far more nuanced than Prothero and begins expanding our conception of what should be included in religious literacy beyond simple facts and figures. There are two essential elements of this definition that are worth highlighting.

First, the focus on "fundamental intersections of religion and social/political and cultural life" is a notably different from Prothero's definition. Rather than focusing on the details of religion, this definition highlights religion as a force that intersects with a broad range of other geopolitical forces. Moore beautifully articulates the downside of basing a definition of religious literacy on facts and figures. She states, "Such an understanding highlights the inadequacy of understanding religions through common means such as learning about ritual practices or exploring 'what scriptures say' about topics or questions."[4] This assertion highlights the functional shortcomings of approaches that focus on religious facts rather than an understanding of the complex relationship between religion, culture, and history that influenced the way these facts developed in the first place.

Second, Moore highlights the importance of not only understanding religion as impacted by global forces, but also as a force of global impact. Moore states: "Critical to this definition is the importance of understanding religions and religious influences in context and as inextricably woven into all dimensions of human experience."[5] Therefore, the importance of religion as a driving force behind cultural developments is essential to the impact of cultural developments on religion, creating a more dynamic framework for placing religion within broader cultural contexts and movements. Moore's definition was adopted by the American Academy of Religions for good reason, and our definition will build upon much of what is highlighted here.

What this definition does not articulate, however, is a vision for the impact that a religiously literate person can have on society and how becoming religiously literate changes an individual's approach to solving real-world problems. Therefore, when developing our own definition of religious literacy, we must ask ourselves: Does developing religious literacy better prepare someone to solve complex geopolitical issues or is it purely an academic pursuit? What would be examples of instances in which a developed religious literacy led to a different outcome? These questions will be central to our definition of religious literacy to ensure that impact and outcomes are always front and center in our conversations about religious literacy.

A third approach to religious literacy is one articulated by Rev. Bud Heckman, Convener of the Interfaith Funders Group. He defines religious literacy as:

> The understanding of 1) the basic tenets of the world's faiths; 2) the diversity of expressions and beliefs within traditions that emerge and evolve in relation to differing social/historical contexts; and 3) the profound role that religion plays in human social, cultural, and political life in both contemporary and historical contexts.[6]

Heckman's definition is a combination of Prothero's and Moore's approaches, but presents a slightly shorter version of the intersection of religion with larger cultural and geopolitical forces. Additionally, Heckman adds a critical component to our discussion: Part of religious literacy is understanding the diversity that is internal to religious groups, not only the diversity of different religions. This notion is stated explicitly by Moore in other places,[7] but Heckman includes this idea in his actual definition of religious literacy in a way not done by other scholars. Diversity within religions is an important piece to any discussion of religious literacy and one that we will highlight again in our approach.

There are a few other important facets that should be considered when discussing religious literacy that have yet to be stated explicitly by any of these definitions. These include the following:

- Thus far, none of these definitions has mentioned the word "ally" or discussed any framework that would demand action and allyship from an individual who is religiously literate.

- The word "knowledge" has appeared in numerous definitions of religious literacy, but we have not distinguished between academic knowledge and experiential knowledge. In other words, is there a difference between the knowledge we can learn from a book or a class and knowledge we can gain by participating in new religious rituals with a friend or classmate?
- None of these definitions of religious literacy has discussed the necessity of self- reflection and the ongoing process of reevaluating one's own beliefs about the world as we come into contact with more difference and diversity. It is rare (or perhaps nearly impossible) for an individual's identity to remain completely static after repeated encounters with diversity, and a framework that accounts for this necessary self-reflection is essential for any complete articulation of religious literacy.

Therefore, to incorporate all of these factors into a single definition and explanation of religious literacy, Global Spiritual Life at NYU has developed the following definition and framework for evaluating religious literacy.

Religious literacy is an understanding of the historic and contemporary interconnections of religion with cultural, political, and social life and the ability to use this knowledge to promote allyship and engage in dialogue on issues of religious or spiritual concern. There are four pillars to religious literacy: knowledge, ecumenical orientation, self-awareness and reflection, and application. These are defined as:

- *Knowledge:* Understanding religious traditions, their diverse historic and contemporary interconnections, and their different effects on local and global communities, cultures, and hierarchies.
- *Ecumenical Orientation:* An interest in developing firsthand experiential knowledge of different religious traditions and an inclination to transverse religio-cultural boundaries.
- *Self-Awareness and Reflection:* Demonstrated insight into the intersection of personal religio-spiritual identity and larger global forces.
- *Application:* A commitment to using religious literacy to inform one's work to bridge intercultural divides.

The most important area to discuss is the definition of religious literacy itself. This definition is heavily influenced by Dianne Moore and her articulation of the interconnection of religion with other global forces. And yet, we have also created a definition of religious literacy that requires action as well as knowledge. In our definition, being religiously literate necessitates putting knowledge into practical use as an ally and by creating space for conversations about religious diversity to flourish. At first glance, allyship and dialogue may seem to be identical manifestations of religious literacy, but there is actually a critical distinction between showing up as an ally and discussing religious differences openly and productively in day-to-day settings. In the first instance, one utilizes religious literacy to attend a rally in support of a colleague who experiences a form of religious discrimination. In the second, one utilizes her position as a manager in her unit to create an environment where people feel comfortable expressing religious identity and asking for religious accommodations as they need. These two manifestations complement each other, but are both equally important to manifesting religious literacy in daily life.

Now that we have a working definition and explanation of religious literacy, it is important to begin analyzing the pillars of religious literacy. These pillars represent the core areas that each person must focus on in his or her process of becoming religiously literate. Each of these four is insufficient by itself, and the combination of the pillars thus represents a holistic approach to developing religious literacy.

The first pillar is knowledge. Our first definition of knowledge, as we highlighted before, is heavily indebted to the work of Dianne Moore. In our explanation, however, we also emphasize an additional clause: "Understanding religious traditions, their diverse historic and contemporary interconnections, and *their different effects on local and global communities, cultures, and hierarchies.*" In this clause, we are highlighting not only the factors of religious literacy left out by Moore, but also the intersection of conversations about religion with conversations about power, privilege, oppression, and hierarchy that are central to so many other diversity conversations. This helps link our workshop to broader diversity conversations students are having on a daily basis, connecting conversations about race, ethnicity, and sexuality to religion and spirituality in powerful and complex ways.

The second pillar is an ecumenical orientation. We have chosen to use the word "ecumenical" rather than more common words and phrases such as "pluralism" or an "orientation toward diversity" because the word ecumenical avoids implications of subjective truths. The word pluralism, used famously by the Pluralism Project at Harvard, is problematic to many students who have religious beliefs that rely on claims of exclusive truth, and who associate pluralism with the implication that all claims must be equally true. This notion is articulated by Ravi Zacharias, founder and President of Ravi Zacharias International Ministries, in an interview with the journal *Enrichment*. He states:

In pluralism you have a competing number of worldviews that are available, and no worldview is dominant. But smuggled in with pluralization was the absolutization of relativism. The only thing we could be sure of was that all moral choices were relative and there was no point of reference to right and wrong. This resulted in the death of reason.[8]

Diana Eck, Founder and Director of the Pluralism Project, is well aware of this phenomenon and articulates a response in her essay "What is pluralism?" She states,

Pluralism is not relativism, but the encounter of commitments. The new paradigm of pluralism does not require us to leave our identities and our commitments behind, for pluralism is the encounter of commitments. It means holding our deepest differences, even our religious differences, not in isolation, but in relationship to one another.[9]

However, because this word is contested, we have decided to rely on the word ecumenism, which, despite its Christian roots, can be used in to refer to all religions. For example, former NYU President John Sexton has used the word ecumenism to describe the project of higher education. On the Multifaithful podcast, Sexton describes ecumenism in the following manner:

Do we want the homogeneity that used to be invoked by the words melting pot in the United States or do we want to embrace the notion that what we are moving to is a second axial age . . . which is a community of communities. And I think the notion of ecumenism has tremendous power in a secular sense when you begin to view it as the building of a community of communities. . . . It's a foreshadowing of what the world could be. . . . So I refer to NYU as the first ecumenical University.[10]

Besides appreciating and adopting an ecumenical attitude toward others, developing this ecumenical orientation requires attaining experiential knowledge of religious identities different from one's own. In other words, to develop a complete understanding of Hinduism, you need to experience some form of Hindu ritual with someone who identifies as Hindu. This is similar to the notion of appreciative knowledge that is used by Eboo Patel, who states:

You need to have an appreciative understanding of other traditions. You need to be able to identify shared values across traditions. How does Islam speak to mercy? How does Christianity speak to mercy? How do Jews speak to mercy? You can do the same with hospitality or service or compassion.[11]

We, however, use the word experiential because we feel that actual experiences and interactions are a critical component in the formation of an ecumenical orientation, not just the development of positive associations and notions about other religions.

The third pillar is self-awareness and reflection. This pillar is one of the most difficult to develop and measure because it requires delving deep into personal insights and approaches to religion and spirituality. Essentially, we want participants to be able to articulate and display an awareness of how an ever-growing exposure to religious ecumenism can also influence one's own religious identity. This does not mean we are hoping for people to become less religious or less secure in their own beliefs. On the contrary, many students actually report a solidification of their beliefs after encountering multifaith experiences. Rather, this pillar requires participants to evaluate how they have developed knowledge from within a particular context, and reflect on how their peers will have done the same. Ultimately, this should provide people with a far more nuanced appreciation of differences in religio-spiritual identity, and perhaps more humility when encountering religio-cultural difference.

The fourth pillar is application. Simply stated, this pillar is the ability of an individual to apply the lessons learned in real-life situations. This is the area in which our definition of religious literacy differs most from many of the other positions elucidated above. We do not feel that religious literacy is a sufficient learning goal without an inclination toward a change in behavior. We will further explore how to measure this learning in the next chapter.

Overall, this approach to religious literacy combines insights from scholars such as Prothero, Moore, and Patel, while providing added insights gleaned from our work at NYU. With this definition in hand, we now must ask the important follow-up question: How do we measure what people are learning? How do we know that our teaching is accomplishing its goals? How do we actually measure religious literacy?

Notes

1 Stephen R. Prothero, *Religious Literacy: What Every American Needs to Know* (San Francisco, CA: Harper San Francisco, 2007), 12.
2 Ibid, 185.
3 Diane Moore, "Overcoming Religious Illiteracy: A Cultural Studies Approach," *World History Connected* 4, no. 1 (2006), http://worldhistoryconnected.press. illinois.edu/4.1/moore.html.
4 Ibid.
5 Ibid.
6 Bud Heckman, "Religious Literacy." *Religion Communicators Council*, accessed March 30, 2016, http://www.religioncommunicators.org/religious-literacy.

7 Diane Moore, "Definition of Religious Literacy," *Religious Literacy Project*, accessed February 23, 2016, http://rlp.hds.harvard.edu/definition-religious-literacy.

8 Ravi Zacharias, "Defending Christianity in a Secular Culture," *RZI*, accessed January 26, 2009, http://rzim.org/just-thinking/defending-christianity-in-a-secular-culture.

9 Diana Eck, "What Is Pluralism," *The Pluralism Project at Harvard University*, 2006, http://pluralism.org/what-is-pluralism/.

10 John Sexton, "God, Baseball and the Spirit of NYU (Part 1)," *Multifaithful Podcast*, November 18, 2015.

11 Eboo Patel, "Eboo Patel: Look to Young People for Leadership in Interfaith Cooperation." *Faith and Leadership*, accessed October 10, 2011, https://www.faithandleadership.com/qa/eboo-patel-look-young-people-for-leadership-interfaith-cooperation.

3 Measuring Religious Literacy

To measure religious literacy, our office spent 2 years developing a rubric for analyzing learning growth along the four pillars of religious literacy mentioned in Chapter 3. In all Faith Zone workshops, we ask students, staff, and faculty to respond to a written prompt asking them to define religious literacy and to articulate its practical uses in their campus context. This rubric is heavily rooted in higher education best practices and existing rubrics for measuring student learning, especially the VALUE Rubric Development Project by the Association of American Colleges. This rubric is the first ever published rubric for measuring religious literacy, and it is one of the most important elements ensuring that our workshop is providing students with the learning they need to become religiously literate.

We have conceptualized growth within this religious literacy rubric as a three-stage process. The first stage is our assumed level of knowledge upon entry to NYU. This assumption is based on survey data that we have collected in workshops over the previous 2 years, and it allows us to articulate the starting point for any student's journey. Second, we have articulated a more advanced level that a participant should reach once they have participated in a Faith Zone session. This represents a reasonable learning expectation for someone attending a single 3-hour workshop and provides us with the foundation for what a student with moderate amount of access to our office would learn over the course of his or her time at NYU. Third, we have a level of knowledge that we expect to be displayed by our student leaders within the Office of Global Spiritual Life and student leaders more broadly. This level is something we do not expect to see as a result of our 3-hour workshops, but it is a goal for how a senior who has been involved in our office for several years might articulate these concepts. Therefore, each time we evaluate students on religious literacy, their grade in a specific pillar should reflect the following values:

- 0 = No Credit (Assumed Pre-Faith Zone Level, Low)
- 1 = Benchmark (Assumed Pre-Faith Zone Level, High)

- 2 = Milestone (Desired Post-Faith Zone Level)
- 3 = Capstone (Desired Level for Student Leaders)

With this foundation, it is now important to explore how each pillar is evaluated by our rubric.

Knowledge

Knowledge is defined as understanding religious traditions and their diverse historic and contemporary interconnections and their different effects on local and global communities, cultures, and hierarchies.[1] The rubric levels for Knowledge are as follows:

Level	Criteria	Example
No Credit (0) [Assumed Pre-Faith Zone]	Can articulate personal or singular knowledge without connections to larger global forces	A statement such as: "I am Jewish, and therefore, fast on Yom Kippur." OR "I know a lot about Islam, because I grew up in Dearborn, Michigan."
Benchmark (1) [Assumed Pre-Faith Zone]	Identifies a basic approach that notes understanding religion without describing specific factors or components of religion as important to understand.	Religion is an important global force.
Milestone (2) [After Faith Zone]	Identifies either: An understanding of religious traditions and their diverse historic and contemporary interconnections and the different effects on local and global communities OR on a systems level, can articulate how cultures can be marked and assigned a place within power structures that determine hierarchies, inequalities, and opportunities and which can vary over time and place, but is unable to demonstrate connections with examples.	Religion is an important global force that manifests itself differently in different contexts throughout the world OR is connected to systems of power and privilege.

(*Continued*)

(Continued)

Level	Criteria	Example
Capstone (3) [Student Leaders]	Demonstrates an understanding of religious traditions, their diverse historic tensions, contemporary interconnections, and effects on local and global communities. On a systems level, can articulate how cultures can be marked and assigned a place within power structures that determine hierarchies, inequalities, and opportunities, varying over time and place.	Religion is an important global force that manifests itself differently in different contexts throughout the world and is connected to systems of power and privilege. For example, someone who is both queer and a religious minority will often feel double marginalization and may have a complex relationship at the intersection of religious and spiritual identity.

Ecumenical[2] Orientation is defined as an interest in developing firsthand experiential knowledge of different religious traditions and an inclination to transverse religio-cultural boundaries. The rubric levels for Ecumenical Orientation area look as follows:

Level	Criteria	Example
No Credit (0) [Assumed Pre-Faith Zone]	Displays no understanding of or orientation toward any form of religious diversity.[3]	No mention of a religious identity other than his or her own
Benchmark (1) [Assumed Pre-Faith Zone]	Expresses attitudes and beliefs with an individualized or singular perspective. Is indifferent or resistant to what can be learned from diversity of communities and cultures.[4]	A personal example such as "I have learned (such and such) from Buddhism and am not interested in other learning."
Milestone (2) [After Faith Zone]	Reflects on how own attitudes and beliefs are different from those of other cultures and communities.[5] Exhibits curiosity about what can be learned from diversity of communities and cultures.[6]	A similar declaration of knowledge from above, but an additional inclination toward learning about others. For example, "Knowing that I have learned (such and such) from Judaism, I would be interested in seeing what other traditions say about this issue and how it impacts adherents."

Level	Criteria	Example
Capstone (3) **[Student Leaders]**	Demonstrates an interest in experiential knowledge of religious traditions and is inclined to traverse religio-cultural boundaries to bridge differences.	Seeking out the opportunity to attend services hosted by a different religious community and involvement and border crossing in different religious communities, ecumenical organizations, or causes.

Self-Awareness and Reflection is defined as demonstrated insight into the intersection of personal religio-spiritual identity and larger global forces. The rubric levels for Self-Awareness and Reflection look as follows:

Level	Criteria	Example
No Credit (0) **[Assumed Pre-Faith Zone]**	Unwilling or unable to describe a personal identity and how it relates to larger global contexts.	A statement that does not indicate a personal identity or how it relates to the topic of religious and spiritual literacy.
Benchmark (1) **[Assumed Pre-Faith Zone]**	Aware of having a spiritual or religious identity and recognition of the impact of their own religious or spiritual identity in a global or local context.	Mentions an identity, but not how it impacts or influences any decisions, preferences, orientations, or opinions.
Milestone (2) **[After Faith Zone]**	Demonstrates a recognition of the origins and influences of one's own religion,[7] cultural heritage, and how this can contribute to a growing sense of interfaith and intercultural identity.	Shows a link between a personal identity and understanding the opinions and identity of others and the histories that accompany their community(ies). For example, "as someone raised as Christian working for Jewish centers, religious literacy is constantly on my mind and conversation and opportunities to learn happen daily."

(Continued)

(Continued)

Level	Criteria	Example
Capstone (3) **[Student Leaders]**	Demonstrates insight into one's own interfaith and intercultural identity as an evolving process. Is able to explain how they process and integrate new knowledge, perspectives, and experiences into their own sense of self.	A statement connecting a cross-cultural experience to a personal change such as, "By participating in a cross-cultural dialogue, I was able to articulate how and when I felt challenged, threatened, and affirmed. I learned that some of the narratives I had been holding were based on false assumptions."

Application is defined as a commitment to using religious literacy to inform one's work to bridge intercultural divides. The rubric levels for Application look as follows:

Level	Criteria	Example
No Credit (0) **[Assumed Pre-Faith Zone]**	Unable to describe any practical applications for the knowledge of religious literacy.	No application described.
Benchmark (1) **[Assumed Pre-Faith Zone]**	Can communicate the importance of working collaboratively across and within civic life to achieve a civic aim[8] and provide solutions to or framing for complex problems in the world, but is not engaged in the work. May be able to list concrete ways to apply this knowledge to individual's work.	Lists concrete actions, but not three of them. Sample concrete actions below.[9]

Level	Criteria	Example
Milestone (2) **[After-Faith Zone]**	Demonstrates interest in engaging in collaborative work across and within civic life and is taking steps to investigate solutions to or framing for complex problems in the world (ending discrimination, bridging intercultural divides, etc.). Able to list three concrete ways to apply this knowledge to individual's work.	Identifies concrete actions (listed below), but may not be personally involved in any of them.
Capstone (3) **[Student Leaders]**	Demonstrates ability, engagement, and commitment to collaborative work across and within civic life[10] and provides solutions to or framing for complex problems in the world (ending discrimination, bridging intercultural divides, etc.).	Creates new and original programs within Global Spiritual Life, such as Muslim Christian Dialogue at NYU.

This rubric contains a layered approach for evaluating religious literacy throughout a college experience. This allows us to track students' growth from their first exposure to our workshops through their development as a student leader in our center.

In aggregate, this new definition of religious literacy and a scaled explanation of growth along its four pillars present a map of how to develop religious literacy and how we can measure its growth. This tool is the foundation for how GSL thinks about our workshops, our student leadership development, and the development of our staff. In future years, we hope to continue publishing updated versions of this rubric as well as our data analysis to evaluate the success of our office. We hope that other centers will do the same so we can advance the field together.

Notes

1 Language utilizing the framework of Diana Moore.
2 Defined by Astin, Astin, and Lindholm as the extent to which the student is interested in different religious traditions, seeks to understand other countries and cultures, feels a strong connection to all humanity.

3   Alyssa Bryant Rockenbach, and Matthew J. Mayhew, "How the Collegiate Religious and Spiritual Climate Shapes Students' Ecumenical Orientation," *Research in Higher Education* 54, no. 4 (2013), 461–479. doi:10.1007/s11162-013-9282-y.

4   "VALUE Rubrics," *Association of American Colleges & Universities*, accessed June 26, 2015, https://www.aacu.org/value-rubrics.

5   Ibid.

6   Ibid.

7   Ibid.

8   Ibid.

9   List created by Global Spiritual Life at NYU includes the following: being aware of dietary needs; keeping track of religious calendars; being respectful of requests made around holidays; being aware of people's comfort with physical contact due to religious observance; making sure that a dress code does not conflict with someone's religious observance; being sensitive of language that can be offensive to a particular religion or to religion in general; being sensitive of imagery that can be offensive to a particular religion or religion in general; allowing those around you to feel safe making religious requests; being able to direct people toward resources for religious and spiritual life; coordinate multifaith events/dialogue amongst constituents; creating/designating spaces for people's religious observances; being able to answer questions people may have about religion; running programming for those seeking religion or spirituality (e.g., Bible study, yoga class); gives me the tools/language to discuss religious and spiritual issues.

10 Defined in Civic Engagement VALUE Rubric as "civic life": the public life of the citizen concerned with the affairs of the community and nation as contrasted with private or personal life, which is devoted to the pursuit of private and personal interests. "VALUE Rubrics." *Association of American Colleges & Universities*.

4   Translating to a Workshop

Now that we have a better sense of religious literacy and how we can measure learning along its pillars, the question becomes how to construct an assessment plan for an individual workshop that is designed to teach religious literacy. To do this, we enter each religious literacy workshop with four learning outcomes. By the conclusion of the workshop, participants should be able to

1. Define religious literacy
2. Explain three concrete areas where religious literacy impacts their work or role at NYU
3. List and explain the resources available through Global Spiritual Life at NYU
4. List religious centers/student groups on campus and explain their relationships to GSL

It is important to note that the levels of evaluation being examined by the rubric are larger than the scope of our actual Faith Zone workshop. This means that unless someone came into the workshop with an incredible degree of knowledge and experience with our office, it would be almost impossible for them to achieve high scores on the questions. This is by design! A 3-hour workshop presents limited opportunities for learning and we have chosen to focus on these learning outcomes and getting participants to at least a level 2 in the different pillars. However, this rubric is intended not only to measure religious literacy in a workshop, but to be used to measure religious literacy for our center as a whole. Therefore, the scores we see on this rubric as it relates to these specific learning outcomes can be lower than people expect.

To measure whether participants achieve these specific learning outcomes, all Faith Zone sessions are accompanied by pre-/post-tests and an evaluation survey to measure satisfaction of participants. These tests ask the following questions:

Pre-/Post-Questions

1. Please define religious literacy and list three concrete ways it impacts your work.
2. Please list three resources available through Global Spiritual Life at NYU.
3. Please list three centers of religious life at NYU.

Evaluation

1. Faith Zone provided a foundation of knowledge needed to facilitate effective dialogue around spiritual issues and concerns. (1–5)

   a. What was most effective?
   b. What was least effective?

2. Faith Zone provided useful tools and information to create a safe and comfortable environment in my interactions across different NYU spaces. (1–5)

   a. What was most effective?
   b. What was least effective?

3. Faith Zone provided a safe environment for useful, structured dialogue and learning around religious and spiritual identities. (1–5)

   a. What was most effective?
   b. What was least effective?

4. Any additional feedback or comments?

Demographic Information (Optional)

1. Race (Check all that apply):
   - ☐ African/African American/Black/Caribbean
   - ☐ Arab/Arab American/Middle Eastern
   - ☐ Asian/Asian American/Pacific Islander
   - ☐ Biracial/Multiracial (please specify): _____
   - ☐ Latino/a
   - ☐ Native American/American Indian/Indigenous

     ☐ White/European American
     ☐ Option not listed: _____

2.   Gender (Check all that apply):
     ☐ Woman
     ☐ Man
     ☐ Transgender
     ☐ Cisgender
     ☐ Gender nonconforming/Genderqueer
     ☐ Option not listed: _____
     ☐ Prefer not to answer

3.   Sexual Orientation (Check all that apply):
     ☐ Lesbian
     ☐ Gay
     ☐ Bisexual/Pansexual
     ☐ Straight
     ☐ Queer
     ☐ Asexual
     ☐ Option not listed: _____
     ☐ Prefer not to answer

4.   Religious Affiliation (Check all that apply):
     ☐ Catholic
     ☐ Protestant
     ☐ Muslim
     ☐ Jewish
     ☐ Atheist
     ☐ Agnostic
     ☐ Buddhist
     ☐ Hindu
     ☐ Humanist
     ☐ Prefer not to answer
     ☐ Spiritual but not religious
     ☐ Other, please specify: _____

This format allows us to gather concrete information that can be loaded into a coded spreadsheet (code book in Appendix B). We analyze these data at the conclusion of every semester and adjust and change our training or materials depending on the feedback we receive.

On the pre-/post-tests, the primary area we are seeking to measure is learning about religious literacy and the resources available to participants on their specific campus. This is reflected in the learning outcomes mentioned at the outset of the chapter, and they are the critical learning elements of these workshops. The evaluation forms, in contrast, enable our team to evaluate the different components of our workshop and update the program depending on the feedback we receive from participants. Over the last few years, there have actually been significant edits to the Faith Zone curriculum based on this feedback, most notably, a complete reshooting of a 30-minute video featuring chaplains from various communities at NYU that was consistently rated as simultaneously the most useful and least useful component of the entire training. This told us that much of the content in the video was crucial to the session, but that we needed to remake the video to increase its effectiveness. There will be more information about this video in the next chapter. Additionally, over the last few years, the amount of time and detail given to various demographic statics about religious and spiritual communities throughout the world has been dramatically reduced in favor of increased time spent on case studies and opportunities for participants to apply new ideas to concrete situations. In fact, the entire second half of the workshop was redesigned within the previous 2 years to account for participants' desire for more ways to discuss practical situations rather than hypothetical conversations.

Now that we have defined religious literacy, explained how it can be measured, and provided materials to conduct this assessment, it is time to discuss a primary question of this book: How do we teach religious literacy in higher education?

Foundations of a Workshop

In each workshop session, we include five components: Setting the Room; Personal Narrative; Unpacking Religious Literacy; Community Snapshot; Next Steps and Takeaways. We will provide sample slides and a facilitators guide in the next chapter, but before delving into the curriculum in such depth, it is key to see how these different components supplement each other and how all five come together for a singular training workshop. These components remain core to all Faith Zone programs, regardless of location or audience. In each section, we will provide a notation that signifies which for the component of the curriculum is being discussed to ensure easy comparison point as you delve through the curriculum. Moreover, for each section, I will suggest replacement and alternative exercises in to allow for more flexibility as people utilize this curriculum to design their own workshops.

Setting the Room

This first section of Faith Zone workshop is common to many diversity workshops, regardless of topic. The key to this section is to create shared rules and expectations among participants to ensure that all subsequent dialogue is conducted honestly and respectfully. To accomplish this, many workshops utilize group guidelines, which can be either generated by the group or provided by a facilitator. Besides the group guidelines, the other central component of this section is to ensure that all participants understand the goals of the workshop and are ready to engage with this topic.

Personal Narrative

This section of Faith Zone is also fairly common to many diversity education workshops and borrows or shares activities that will be familiar to many readers. Activities such as the name story, early memories, or other personal reflection activities allow participants to begin unpacking their own personal experiences with the topic at hand. This should enable participants to begin understanding the connection between their own beliefs and experiences and how they approach the topic at hand.

Unpacking Religious Literacy

This section of Faith Zone is where the workshop begins to present content that is not group-generated. Until now, the group has been learning through discussion and reflection with guidance from the facilitator. Now, however, the workshop turns to the concept of religious literacy and begins to explain some of the concepts that have already been discussed in this book. The exact exercises and methods we use to teach this topic will be explained in the curriculum in the next chapter.

Community Snapshot

After analyzing religious literacy, it is critical to spend time discussing specific local communities and resources available to each religious and spiritual group. At NYU, we accomplish this through a video with our chaplains, but this can be done in any number of ways that would ask participants to think about their community members, who is represented in positions of leadership, and how to think about representations in the most equitable way possible.

Next Steps and Takeaways

The final step in the training is for participants to begin translating what they have learned into concrete action steps that can be brought to their specific roles in a community. We do this through various action plans and tips, but there are numerous ways to engineer these exercises. The key focus here should be concrete and actionable takeaways so that participants leave with actions they know can be taken immediately.

These different components will remain present in the next chapter as we move through a sample Faith Zone curriculum. Each section will be noted at the top of the page and presented with alternative exercises to ensure that each part of this curriculum can be replicated as easily as possible at each campus.

5   Sample Workshop

SETTING THE ROOM

Slide 1

 NYU

INTRODUCTION TO RELIGIOUS AND SPIRITUAL LITERACY

welcome! PLEASE FILL OUT THE PRE-TEST BEFORE WE BEGIN

Transition: Welcome and introduction from facilitator

Important Points

- Welcome to Faith Zone
- Name and role on campus
- Please make sure you have filled out your pre-test.

Final Thought:

To make sure that evaluation is conducted successfully, we occasionally need to sacrifice a few minutes of workshop time at the outset to ensure participants complete the pre-test.

Slide 2

INTRODUCTIONS
▬

AROUND THE ROOM

Introduce yourself:

Why did you come today?

Does awareness about religious and spiritual diversity
influence your work?

Transition: Everyone should introduce themselves and begin discussing
their connection to the topic at hand. This workshop is best taught by two
co-facilitators who have different religious or spiritual identities, but can be
taught by a single experienced facilitator if necessary.

Important Points
- Everyone introduce yourself with your name and role on campus.
- Why did you come today? What about Faith Zone interests you?
- Any first impressions about how learning more about this topic will
  help you in your day-to-day work?

Final Thought:
If the group is larger than 30, consider breaking people up into groups of 5–6
and then having everyone report back.

Slide 3

AGENDA

- Goals and Group Guidelines
- Name Story and Personal Reflections
- Religious Literacy—What is it?
- Data on Religion and Spirituality
- Film
- Break!
- Case Studies
- Personal Action Plan
- Tips for Dialogue and Closing

Transition: Before we dive in, we wanted to lay out the agenda for today so that you have a sense of where we will go with our conversation.

Important Points
- Read through the agenda
- Bracket all conversations about religious literacy: This is the crux of our later discussion, and we will get into it then.

Final Thought:

This should be a relatively quick slide.

Slide 4

TODAY'S GOALS

REFLECT on the role that religion and spirituality may play in our lives.

EXPLORE how developing religious and spiritual literacy can prepare us to work in diverse environments.

DISCUSS the different religious and spiritual communities at NYU and the resources available to them through Global Spiritual Life.

Transition: We want to be extremely clear about our goals for today and what we can hope to learn.

Important Points

- *Reflect:* The first step in our conversation is to unpack the personal. What is my relationship to this topic? How does that influence how I will approach others?
- *Explore:* Buzzword alert! We will define and explore religious literacy later so we are going to leave it for now. But remember it's the frame for everything we will discuss today.
- *Discuss:* We will make sure to discuss the resources available on your campus and some action steps for utilizing them as effectively as possible.

Final Thought:

The next slide of "not goals" is just as important as the goals.

Slide 5

FAITH ZONE

▬

IS NOT a chance to take introduction to all world religions in one session

NOR is it an opportunity to discuss the merits of faith and belief.

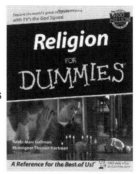

Transition: If we are going to be clear about what Faith Zone is, then it is equally important to be clear about what Faith Zone is not.

Important Points

- An introduction to all world religions in 3 hours is both impossible and unhelpful. It does not tell you how to best approach someone who has a different religious or spiritual identity.
- The merits of faith and belief are an important topic for understanding religion, but we don't have time to discuss them in 3 hours. That can be Faith Zone 4, but for now we are going to have to table it.

Final Thought:

People may have questions about why they are not going to learn about the details of different religions. It is important to emphasize that details about religious observance are important to learn, but on a macro level, it is more important to develop comfort talking about these issues and learning how to approach someone different than you. That is the primary focus we will be taking. If you are interested in trainings that contain details about various religions, we encourage you to make use of the resources available through Harvard Universities Religious Literacy Project and the Tannenbaum Center for Interreligious Understanding.[1,2]

Slide 6

GROUP GUIDELINES

- Use "I" statements whenever possible.
- Be present.
- Monitor your participation and adjust accordingly. Move in, move out.
- Maintain confidentiality regarding other people's stories, but share new information, facts, etc.
- Take a risk and have fun!

Transition: One last important note before we begin. Group guidelines are an important part of diversity conversations because they help set ground-rules for communication that we will use throughout the session.

Important Points

- These are only a sample of group guidelines and facilitators should allow the group to add or subtract as they see fit.
- **Use "I" Statements whenever possible.** Describe your own experience without generalizing to entire groups. Give an example, such as "In my experience as a Jewish person . . ." rather than "Judaism says . . ."
- **Be present.** If you start to disengage from the conversation, people can read that as being disinterested or disrespectful.
- **Monitor your participation and adjust accordingly. Move in, move out.** Determine whether you're a quieter or more expressive person, and try to either stretch beyond your comfort zone or rein it in so that more people's voices can be heard.
- **Maintain confidentiality regarding other people's stories, but share new information, facts, etc.** Keep personal stories confidential, while still taking away the lessons and information learned in the session.

Final Thought:

The end of this slide should be around 20 minutes into the workshop.

Alternate Exercises

If you are interested in adding additional resources to the "setting the room" portion of the workshop, there are numerous resources that provide more extensive group guidelines and activities that can help set the stage for a productive dialogue. One of the best resources is *Teaching for Diversity and Social Justice* (especially page 54) as well as the websites for organizations such as Free Minds, Free People, The Religion Communicators Council, and The Center for Research on Learning and Teaching at the University of Michigan.[3,4,5,6]

PERSONAL NARRATIVE

Slide 7

WHAT IS YOUR NAME STORY?

—

- What is the history of your name?
  first, middle, and last

- What is the significance of your name?
  Are you named for someone? Does your name have a translation or another meaning?

- What role, if any, did a religious or spiritual tradition play in your name story?

Transition: Lets jump in! Let's start by unpacking our own religious or spiritual journey and how it might relate to this topic.

Important Points:
- This activity should be done in groups of 2–3, with each person having at least 3 to 5 minutes to share his or her name story and respond to follow-up questions.
- This is a very common diversity education exercise. Some people might have done it before. If that is you, try to focus on any spiritual dimensions to your name story that you may not have discussed last time.
- If you have no religious or spiritual component to your name, that's not a problem! Discuss why you might not have those elements.
- Facilitators should share their own name story in 1 minute before asking people to begin their pair-share.
- After each group has finished, the facilitator should reconvene the groups. Ask participants what they learned. Did their group talk about something unexpected?
- This slide and the next slide together should be 20 minutes

Final Thought:

Things to keep in mind—Sometimes this activity can touch on family or social trauma such as adopted names, names that owe their history to slavery or colonialization and given/chosen names of trans participants. Make sure to preface the conversation by mentioning this and offering anyone the option not to share if they are not comfortable.

Slide 8

RELIGIOUS AND SPIRITUAL MEMORIES

▬

ONE

What is your earliest memory of having, or not having, a particular religious affiliation or identity?

TWO

How did you negotiate your religious or spiritual identity, if at all, in high school through your current stage of life?

Transition: Now that we have begun unpacking some of our own family history in this area, let's move forward to discussing our own religious or spiritual trajectories. We will begin with a question that focuses on our childhoods and then one that focuses on high school (the point where many of us began to make decisions about our identity) and finish with today.

Important Points

- This exercise should follow the same guidelines and timing as the previous one. Keep the groups as small as possible to give people more time to talk.
- Switch up the groups from the previous exercise.

Final Thought:

The key here is to have the participants unpack how their experiences may influence their interactions with others.

Alternate Exercises

There are many other ways to spur conversations about spiritual journeys. One of the most common, and one that I have used in Faith Zone sessions before, is a life mapping exercise that asks participants to draw a few images representing different stages of their lives, and then explain these images in small groups. Alternatively, Marshall Ganz, Professor of Public Policy at the John F. Kennedy School of Government at Harvard University, has popularized a public narratives workshop called "Telling Your Public Story: Self, Us, Now."[7] Elements of this workshop can extremely effective for helping participants develop their personal stories into coherent narratives that are easily communicable to other members of the workshop. The entire exercise generally takes much longer than the time we have allotted in our Faith Zone workshops, but in smaller doses, it can be an effective tool for developing and communicating a personal narrative.

UNPACKING RELIGIOUS LITERACY

Slide 9

BRAINSTORM TERMS

What words do you associate with RELIGION?

What words to you associate with SPIRITUALITY?

Transition: Now that we have begun to unpack the personal, it is important for us to begin creating a working language for us to use when discussing our topic today. To that end, lets unpack the words religion and spirituality.

Important Points

- This activity is best done by staggering the prompts for religion and spirituality in the presentation so that participants don't know they will be asked to compare the two.
- Begin by putting the word religion on the board and prompting the group to throw out words they identify with religion, both positive and negative.
- Do the same exercise with spirituality.
- Once the board has words for both concepts, compare and contrast the lists and see what impressions people have. Some trends that you might see:
    - People have a much easier time coming up with negative words for religion than spirituality.
    - Religion is often associated with institutions, whereas spirituality is often associated with personal beliefs.

- It is often more difficult for the group to list words for spirituality while they can easily list 30 words or more when talking about religion.
- A typed-up version of this activity after a session at NYU can be found in Appendix C.

Final Thought:

Ask the group whether doing this activity would yield different results if conducted in a different environment. Would a group from China or India give the same sets of words? Why? This will begin to get the group thinking about the relationship between our associations with these words and culture, history, and politics.

Slide 10

BRAINSTORM

HOW WOULD YOU DEFINE "RELIGION"?

An organized community of faith that has written doctrine and codes of regulatory behavior.[8]

The belief in and worship of a superhuman controlling power, especially a personal God or gods.[9]

A particular system of faith; a pursuit or interest followed with great devotion.[10]

Transition: Part of the complication we just experienced when coming up with these words is that there is actually no single accepted definition of religion or of spirituality!

Important Points

- Each of these definitions has serious weaknesses.
- Do all religions have structured communities and written codes guiding behavior?
- Do all religious people believe in God?
- Wouldn't a pursuit or interest followed with great devotion work equally well to describe my relationship with the Green Bay Packers?

Final Thought:

This slide should be done relatively quickly. The goal is not to create our own definition and debate the merits of each definition. We simply want to highlight how none is perfect.

Slide 11

BRAINSTORM

HOW WOULD YOU DEFINE "SPIRITUALITY"?

Meaning-making, how people construct their lives and move towards authenticity.[11]

Relating to or affecting the human spirit or soul as opposed to material or physical.[12]

Of relating to religion or religious beliefs.[13]

Transition: We see the same picture with spirituality.

Important Points

- The first definition is beautiful, but why is this spirituality and not religion?
- Do all spiritual people believe in the dichotomy between body and soul? What about people who do Yoga as a spiritual practice?
- Not helpful at all

Final Thought:

The terms at our disposal are complicated and confusing.

Slide 12

RELIGIOUS LITERACY

▬

Religious literacy is understanding the historic and contemporary interconnections of religion with cultural, political, and social life and the ability to use this knowledge to promote allyship and engage in dialogue on issues of religious or spiritual concern.

—Global Spiritual Life at NYU

Transition: How do we develop a working language for talking about this topic that can explain how we approach conversations about religious and spiritual identity?

Important Points

- There is no one accepted definition of religious literacy out there. In fact, you can find at least four of five if you search on Google.
- This is the definition we created ourselves, based on these other definitions, because it best captures what we think is important to learn.
- Unpack this definition with the room. What is this definition saying? What is it not saying? (This is explained in detail in Chapter 3.)

Final Thought:

Utilize Chapter 3 of this book for details on this definition.

Alternate Exercises

The structure of this section has generally remained constant throughout various Faith Zone workshops, but one alternative that has been successful is to give participants different definitions of religious literacy on a worksheet, and have them analyze the similarities and differences between each definition. This is a text-study exercise, and it forces participants to evaluate what they find important in each definition. This type of exercise will only be successful with a longer time-span than we typically allot for this section, but further meditation on the various definitions of religious literacy could be useful, especially for a more advanced group.

COMMUNITY SNAPSHOT

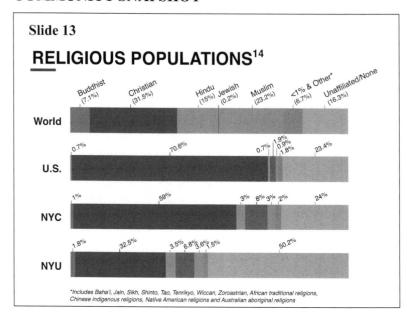

Slide 13

RELIGIOUS POPULATIONS[14]

Transition: If religious literacy is our framework for understanding religious diversity, the question becomes: Who are the members of our community that we meet on a regular basis, and how does this representation correspond to communities throughout the world?

Important Points

- The key idea here is to layer religious populations from a global–local context so that people understand why they know more about certain religious groups than others.
- In the United Sates, which populations are growing and which are not? Why might that be?
- Data slides (next three) should be 15 minutes

Final Thought:

There are a few general points that always generate surprise when presented. They are the following:

- The percentage of Jewish people being so small
- What is the difference between Atheist, Agnostic, and none?

- How to decide who gets highlighted and who is lumped into a single category?
- All of these surveys are self-identification, and they ask people to choose how they identify: It says nothing about levels of religiosity or changing beliefs.
- Also, people did not have the options to write in more than one response (people from multifaith families, for example).

Slide 14

HIGHER EDUCATION[15]

Have an interest in spirituality	81%
Believe in the sacredness of life	84%
My spirituality is a source of joy	64%
Searching for meaning/purpose in life	76%
Discuss meaning of life with friends	74%

Transition: In the 1970s and 1980s, it was in vogue to say that religion was disappearing from higher education. This has been proven false.

Important Points

- Astin and Astin studies provide the foundation for much of student affairs.
- Ask the room—are these numbers surprising? Is this reflective of the students you encounter?

Final Thought:

Ask people to think about the nature of their institution and why their numbers may be different than above. Would the numbers at NYU be the same as Notre Dame?

Slide 15
HIGHER EDUCATION[16]

Attend religious services	81%
Believe in God	79%
Pray	69%
Religious beliefs: strength, support, guidance	68%
Follow religious teaching in everyday life	40%

Transition: This slide is a continuation of the trend highlighted in the previous slide. It provides even more evidence and context for the significance of religious and spiritual discussions to American college students.

Important Points:
• This comes from the same study as before.
• Ask the room similar questions: Are these numbers surprising? Is this reflective of the students you encounter?

Final Thought:
Just as the previous slide, ask people to think about the nature of their institution and why their numbers may be different than above. Would the numbers at NYU be the same as Notre Dame?

Slide 16
Chaplain Video

Transition: Now that we have learned about ourselves, religious literacy and some broader demographic trends, the question becomes how do we work with the people in our community? What are the areas to which we should be most attentive? What are the particular religious or spiritual needs of our students?

Important Points

- Interviews with our chaplains
- They were asked to discuss: What are important pieces of information for Student Affairs professionals to know when working with your student population?
- This does not come close to covering everything and is meant to be an introduction to topics and types of considerations that are important when working with religious or spiritual student populations.
- Often, people love this video except for the part where a chaplain is discussing the viewer's own religion! We know that this film does not convey the full internal complexity and diversity of all these groups.
- Video is 30 minutes long.

Final Thought:

On to the break!

Alternate Exercises

It is often extremely difficult to find accurate data on religious populations on college campuses. These questions are often not asked by campus climate surveys, and it can be difficult to present the information in the same layered way we have presented it above. Moreover, not every campus will have access to the resources that are necessary to make a similar video, making it difficult to present a broad spectrum of student needs and considerations in the same way. As a replacement, bringing in panels of students or campus religious leaders to discuss their respective communities and to present a few areas of concern for their group can be effective. This section is often the most difficult to replicate because it is so heavily dependent on local resources, which can vary widely from campus to campus.

NEXT STEPS AND TAKEAWAYS

Slide 17

CASE STUDIES: WHEN IT GETS COMPLICATED

▬▬

1. You are organizing an overnight trip for a group of students. What are some areas of religious observance that may require accommodation and foreplaning?

2. Recently, political candidates running for office in your area have made comments that are interpreted as threatening to a specific community. What are a few steps you can take in your community to mitigate people feeling threatened?

3. You are in charge of organizing a holiday party in December. Discuss the steps you would take to make this party inclusive.

Transition: Now that we have discussed a framework and some areas to be aware of when working in this area, it's time to dive into some practical case studies and begin applying our knowledge.

Important Points:

Each case study should be discussed in groups of 3–4 for 10 minutes. The group should then report back for 5 minutes. A few points for the case studies we have chosen:

- The major areas that people should discuss are gender as it relates to sleeping assignments, food options on the trip, travel days/times and days of worship and social activities that may occur in places where participants are uncomfortable (for example, many Muslim students may be uncomfortable getting drinks at the local bar).
- This case study is designed to get people to think about allyship and how broader political trends can have an impact on local communities. The groups should discuss the value of making big public statements or more private outreach. Should people post support from social media accounts?

- Which religious traditions should be represented? How do you approach including groups who may not have a holiday at this time? What about groups that do not have clear symbols or imagery?

Final Thought:

There are many ways to teach case studies and to structure this section, depending on your particular needs. These are meant to be general guiding questions, but each of these could be a longer discussion in its own right. Occasionally, we will substitute a single case study rather than a set of smaller ones.

Slide 18

PERSONAL ACTION PLAN

Four questions:

• How is religious literacy important in my role on campus?

• In what areas have we yet to consider religious and spiritual needs within my sphere of influence?

• Who from my network, both at NYU and beyond, might be helpful in this area?

• Is there anything covered today that is immediately useful?

Transition: This slide will be given as a handout. In the same groups as the previous slide fill out the four questions (changed for your particular community).

Important Points:

This slide is the opportunity for people to begin thinking of concrete steps they can take, given the resources available on their campus.

Final Thought:

Make sure people write down responses to these questions! The process of writing and taking it home will make it more likely that the ideas will stick.[17]

Slide 19

10 Tips for Religious Literacy

ONE

Refer to GSL Principles of Multifaith Engagement

a. Reflect diversity, accounting for the complex and intersectional identities of our constituents.
b. Rooted in face-to-face encounters and deep relationship building within and between communities and/or individuals.
c. Committed to social transformation and civic engagement
d. Focused on introspection and meaning-making as a way of understanding spirituality.
e. Inclusive of and attentive to personal narratives through intentional storytelling pedagogy
f. Supportive of the integration of the whole student experience throughout their academic and co-curricular development.
g. Supportive of coursework that promotes multifaith leadership.

Transition: GSL at NYU has also written a list of 10 tips that should be helpful for utilizing religious literacy.

Important Points:

1. This first slide is less a tip for practical work and more about an ethical foundation for our work that was co-written by students, staff, and chaplains.

Final Thought:

This slide is very text heavy, so avoid reading it out loud. Providing a handout for all 10 tips can be helpful so people can take it home.

Slide 20

10 Tips for Religious Literacy

——

TWO
Create a safe space that encourages dialogue. Approach every conversation with a co-learner orientation.

THREE
Ask people about their personal practices. Not all people within a religious or spiritual community practice in the same way.

FOUR
Don't be afraid of making mistakes. Let those around you know that they can voice a concern if something you say offends them.

Transition: Continue going through the tips one by one, asking different people to read them out loud and explain for the room.

Important Points:

A few pieces of guidance for these tips:

2. "Co-learner" is one of our student affairs buzzwords. Feel free to change the language to fit your context.
3. It is important to recognize the diversity that is internal to religious groups.
4. This one is really important: You will make mistakes! Don't be afraid and make sure to own them.

Final Thought:

Giving personal examples of mistakes you have made as a facilitator and how you have dealt with it can be helpful here.

Slide 21

10 Tips for Religious Literacy

FIVE

Whenever possible, organizers should always reflect the diversity of those who will be participating.

SIX

Events should be easily accessible and comfortable for all potential participants. Some things to consider:
   a. Religious holidays (available on Google Calendar)
   b. Prayer times

SEVEN

At an event itself, ensure that the structure of the event is inclusive. Some things to consider:
   a. Dietary needs such as Kosher, Halal, vegetarian, vegan, etc.
   b. Physical contact between genders

Transition: Continue going through the tips one by one and asking different people to read them out loud and explain for the room.

Important Points:

A few pieces of guidance for these tips:

5. This helps us avoid problems such as tokenizing or having speakers that do not represent the intended community.
6. Everything you need for holidays is available as an add-on to your Google calendar. This makes holidays that are not always on the same secular calendar dates (such as Ramadan) easy to remember.
7. If you are unsure about the physical contact, do not extend your hand first! Wait for the other person to indicate their preference.

Final Thought:

Numbers 6 and 7 are probably the best quick takeaways for people to come away from the session remembering.

Slide 22

10 Tips for Religious Literacy

EIGHT

Create an environment where people feel safe making requests for religious and spiritual observance or practice. Make it clear that there will not be ramifications for making that request.

NINE

Use of inclusive language to welcome students who do not identify with a particular faith tradition or identify as atheist or agnostic.

TEN

Seek help or advice from chaplains and other resources!

Transition: Continue going through the tips one by one and asking different people to read them out loud and explain for the room.

Important Points:

A few pieces of guidance for these tips:

8. This is especially important for professors. Make it clear that students should mention possible conflicts as early in the semester as possible so that you can account for it.
9. This is hard to do for religious people. Remember, non-theists are often involved in our programs and deserve to be included!
10. Make a plug for your own community resources.

Final Thought:

Making sure people leave knowing the resources that are already available to them is critical.

Alternate Exercises

This component of the workshop is the one that most easily lends itself to alternative exercises. There are many different tools available that can help encourage participants to think more deeply about religious literacy. For example, the case studies written by the Pluralism Project at Harvard University are some of the best practical learning tools available for questions dealing with religious diversity. These case studies cover a wide range of topics and are fantastic for groups that want to dedicate long sessions to a single case example. Additionally, *A Guidebook of Promising Practices: Facilitating College Students' Spiritual Development* contains an entire appendix with a sample campus questionnaire that can be used to evaluate the current campus environment. Either of these sources provides ample replacement activities and can be used to varying degrees, depending on the needs of your particular group.

Slide 23

GLOBAL SPIRITUAL LIFE AT NYU

———

- *Faith Zone*
- *Minor in Multifaith and Spiritual Leadership*
- *"Multifaithful" Podcast*
- *"Of Many" Film*
- *Student Multifaith Advisory Council*

- *Twice-Daily Yoga Classes*
- *Meditation Classes*
- *Mindfulness in Business*
- *Mindfulness Retreats*
- *Meditation Room*

- *Chaplains' Circle*
- *Bronfman Center for Jewish Student Life*
- *Catholic Center at NYU*
- *Islamic Center at NYU*
- *Protestant Life Affiliate Network (PLAN)*

Transition: At NYU, this is how religious and spiritual life is organized.

Important Points:

The details of this slide were covered in Chapter 1.

Final Thought:

It may be a good idea to consider making a similar slide for your own campus.

Slide 24
NYU IN THE ZONE

Transition: At NYU, we care deeply about diversity education and market all our workshops together.

Important Points:

We have the following:

- **Safe Zone** is a campus-wide program designed to visibly identify students, staff, and faculty peers who support the LGBTQ population, understand some of the issues facing LGBTQ individuals, and are aware of the various LGBTQ resources. This 3-hour training session provides a foundation of knowledge needed to be an effective ally to LGBTQ students and those questioning their sexuality.[18]
- **Diversity Zone** explores issues that surround race and racism. Open to students, staff, and faculty, Diversity Zone provides participants with tools and information on the roots, construction, and proliferation of social identities as well as with a basic understanding of the systems of power, privilege and oppression at work in our society. Participants examine intersections across systems of oppression (such as racism and classism), connect issues of diversity and social justice to their everyday lives, and learn ways to practice better allyship.[19]
- **Action Zone** is a bystander intervention training for risk reduction adapted from the University of Arizona's *Step UP!* program. Studies

show that in emergency situations most people present would like to help, but very few actually do. Action Zone explores this phenomenon—The Bystander Effect—as well as when to intervene and when not to. Often, sexual assaults, alcohol-fueled incidents, and other challenging situations can be prevented or diffused with timely, skilled, and appropriate intervention. This dynamic, interactive training prepares participants to be allies in the NYU community.[20]

- **DREAM Zone** is an interactive training designed to explore the basic issues that surround the undocumented community, with a focus on undocumented students. DREAM Zone provides students, staff and faculty with a basic review of federal and local policies, discusses some of the issues undocumented students face specifically at NYU, and explores ways in which to be a better advocate and ally and create a more inclusive and supportive campus environment.[21]
- **Disability Zone** offers a framework for engaging and discussing disability justice. Participants will learn about the spectrum and subjectivity of disability status; review terminology, language, policy, and NYU resources; discuss accessibility needs; and explore best practices for allyship.[22]

Final Thought:

This slide will look different on every campus, but bringing further recognition to other opportunities for education is a perfect conclusion to Faith Zone.

Slide 25

BEFORE YOU LEAVE TODAY

ONE

Complete the post-test.

TWO

Fill out the evaluation and intake form.

THREE

Receive your Faith Zone certification.

Transition: Thanks for coming and we hope you enjoyed!

Important Points:

Make sure you fill out the assessment forms and get your certificate. The certificate is a nice incentive to make sure that folks fill out the assessment forms.

Final Thought:

It can be helpful to stress to participants that every single piece of feedback is read and taken seriously. This is the best way to make sure your training is always evolving and improving.

Notes

1 World Religions Through Their Scriptures," *EdX*, accessed March 21, 2016, https://www.edx.org/xseries/world-religions-through-scriptures.
2 "Curricula for Educators," *Tanenbaum Center for Religious Understanding*, accessed March 30, 2016, https://tanenbaum.org/https://tanenbaum.org/product-category/curricula/.
3 Maurianne Adams, Lee Anne Bell, and Pat Griffin, *Teaching for Diversity and Social Justice: A Sourcebook* (New York, NY: Routledge, 1997).

4   "Guidelines for Healthy Dialogue," *Free Minds Free People*, accessed November 1, 2016, https://fmfp.org/about/guidelines-for-healthy-dialogue/.

5   "Guidelines for Interfaith Dialogue," *Religion Communicators Council*, accessed November 1, 2016, http://www.religioncommunicators.org/guidelines-for-interfaith-dialogue.

6   "Guidelines for Discussing Difficult or Controversial Topics," *Center for Research on Learning and Teaching*, accessed November 1, 2016, http://www.crlt.umich.edu/publinks/generalguidelines.

7   Marshall Ganz, "Telling Your Public Story: Self, Us, Now," 2007, https://philstesthomepage.files.wordpress.com/2014/05/public-story-worksheet07ganz.pdf.

8   Elizabeth Tisdell, *Exploring Spirituality and Culture in Adult and Higher Education* (San Francisco: Jossey-Bass, 2003).

9   "Religion," *Oxford Dictionaries*, https://en.oxforddictionaries.com/definition/religion.

10   Ibid.

11   Elizabeth Tisdell, "The Connection of Spirituality to Culturally Responsive Teaching in Higher Education," *Spirituality in Higher Education* 1, no. 4 (2004): 1–9, http://spirituality.ucla.edu/docs/newsletters/1/Tisdell.pdf.

12   "Spirituality," *Oxford Dictionaries*, https://en.oxforddictionaries.com/definition/spiritual.

13   "Spirituality," *Merriam-Webster*, http://www.merriam-webster.com/dictionary/spirituality.

14   "Religious Affiliation of New York Residents by Borough," *PRRI*, accessed September 22, 2015, http://www.prri.org/spotlight/religious-affiliation-of-new-york-residents-by-borough/.

15   Astin, Astin, and Lindholm, *Cultivating the Spirit*, 39.

16   Ibid, 83.

17   Adapted from J. A. Lindholm, *A Guidebook of Promising Practices: Facilitating College Students' Spiritual Development* (Oakland: Regents of the University of California, 2011).

18   "SafeZone: NYU's Ally Program," *New York University*, http://www.nyu.edu/students/communities-and groups/student-diversity/lesbian-gay-bisexual-transgender-and-queer-student-center/education-advocacy-and-trainings/safezone.html.

19   "Zone Trainings," *New York University*, https://www.nyu.edu/students/communities-and-groups/student-diversity/multicultural-education-and-programs/what-we-do/social-justice-education/zone-trainings.html.

20   "Action Zone Bystander Intervention," *New York University*, http://www.nyu.edu/students/health-and-wellness/student-health-center/programs-events/action-zone.html.

21   "Zone Trainings," *New York University*.

22   Ibid.

6 Workshop Outcomes

Now that we have explored much of the theoretical and pedagogical foundation for teaching religious literacy, we can delve into the measurable outcomes we have observed at NYU since the inception of the original Faith Zone curriculum in 2012. In Chapter 5, we articulated the various learning outcomes and assessment questions that were necessary to evaluate a Faith Zone workshop. Our intended learning outcomes are that participants should be able to define religious literacy; explain three concrete areas where religious literacy impacts their work; list and explain at least three resources available through Global Spiritual Life at NYU; list three religious centers/ student groups on campus. These responses are collected in both pre- and post-tests, and graded with a rubric to measure learning. In addition, at the conclusion of every Faith Zone, participants are asked to rank the session on a scale of 1 to 5 in three different assessment categories, while identifying which components of the workshop were most effective and least effective (the exact questions appear in the assessment materials presented in Chapter 5). The insight gleaned from these sections is the first step in discussing concrete outcomes based on Faith Zone workshop sessions.

Thus far, the data we have collected on Faith Zone (since its first pilot sessions in 2012) have yielded the following results.[1]

- 83.57 percent of participants agreed or strongly agreed that "Faith Zone provided a foundation of knowledge needed to facilitate effective dialogue around spiritual issues and concerns." This number is over 90 percent in the 2016–2017 academic year.
- 83.96 percent of participants agreed or strongly agreed that "Faith Zone provided useful tools and information to create a safe and comfortable environment in my interactions across different NYU spaces." This number is over 88 percent in the 2016–2017 academic year.
- 89.6 percent of participants agreed or strongly agreed that "Faith Zone provided a safe environment for useful, structured dialogue and

learning around religious and spiritual identities." This number is over 96 percent in the 2016–2017 academic year.

- Awareness of religious centers at NYU increased over 45 percent as a result of a Faith Zone workshop, with participants being able to list an average 2.64 (out of 3) centers on their post-tests.
- Awareness of programs being run by the office of Global Spiritual Life at NYU increased over 50 percent as a result of a Faith Zone workshop, with participants being able to list an average of 2.69 (out of 3) programs on their post-tests.
- Since the implementation of this current rubric in the summer of 2016, we have seen an increase in measured religious literacy of over 47 percent. Our average post-test rubric score is a 5.54 (out of an ideal score of 8 for a post-Faith Zone workshop). The scores are broken down as:

  - Knowledge: 1.82/2
  - Ecumenical Orientation: 1.49/2
  - Self-Awareness and Reflection: .44/2
  - Diversity: 1.79/2

What is clear from this data is that participants are scoring extremely highly on 3 out of 4 metrics, displaying high levels of knowledge and growth toward a rubric score of 2. The lone exception is the Self-Awareness category. These scores are consistently lower than the other categories, indicating the need to focus more heavily on this pillar during the workshops and ensure that this concept is being more accurately communicated to the participants. Overall, however, we are extremely pleased with these data and feel that it clearly shows that Faith Zone has been overwhelmingly successful in meeting our learning outcomes and communicating a complex and nuanced approach toward religious literacy to participants.

Utilizing the Rubric

Now that we have given an overview of our most recent data collections from Faith Zone, it is important to demonstrate how to utilize the rubric to evaluate participant responses. To illustrate this, we have included two examples, below, of responses to our pre-/post-test prompt: "Please define religious literacy and discuss three ways it impacts your work."

As a reminder, each score in the grade column bellow corresponds to:

- 0 = No Credit (Assumed Pre-Faith Zone Level, Low)
- 1 = Benchmark (Assumed Pre-Faith Zone Level, High)
- 2 = Milestone (Desired Post-Faith Zone Level)
- 3 = Capstone (Desired Level for Student Leaders)

Example 1

Student pre-test free written response: Being respectful and aware of various religions.

(1) Respect students' religious experiences/preferences.
(2) _____
(3) _____

Category	Grade	Reason
Knowledge	1	Identifies religion as a concept but without specifying which components of religion are important to understand and account for.
Ecumenical Orientation	2	Indicates an interest in learning about religious and spiritual identities that are different from their own.
Self-Awareness and Reflection	0	No discussion of a personal identity and its connection to the topic.
Application	1	Only lists one concrete application.

Student post-test free written response: Understanding the historic and contemporary influences of religion and having dialogue about issues of different communities.

(A) Understanding interfaith issues in our NYC/NYU community
(B) Current politics making targeted communities feel safe
(C) BLANK

Category	Grade	Reason
Knowledge	2	Identifies historic and contemporary influences of religion in diverse contexts.
Ecumenical Orientation	2	Expresses the importance of learning about other communities and interfaith relationships.
Self-Awareness and Reflection	0	No discussion of personal identity and its connection to the topic.
Application	1	Only lists two applications, not the required three.

By comparing these two responses through the lens of a rubric, we can articulate that this student moved from a grade of 4 on the pre-test to a grade of 5 on the post-test. This yields a growth of 1. A post-test score of 5, though respectable, is not in the ideal score zone (an ideal post-Faith Zone score would be an 8).

Example 2

Staff Pre: The understanding and vocabulary to speak of religions and their beliefs.

(1) _____

(2) _____

(3) _____

Category	Grade	Reason
Knowledge	1	Religion as a global force or as concept hinted to but not articulated directly.
Ecumenical Orientation	0	No mention of a diversity of religious identities
Self-Awareness and Reflection	0	No discussion of personal identity
Application	0	No practical uses listed

Staff Post: Understanding historic and contemporary context of religion, how it impacts social cultural and political aspects of daily lives while promoting allyship and dialogue.

(1) Student Support

(2) Accommodation of office events

(3) Cultural understanding (differences and similarities)

Category	Grade	Reason
Knowledge	3	Gives an almost word-for-word perfect definition.
Ecumenical Orientation	2	Mentions the importance of being accommodating and open to others and studying cultural differences.
Self-Awareness and Reflection	2	Mention of allyship and linking the personal to working with other communities.
Application	2	Lists three practical applications

In this example, we clearly see someone who did not spend the time and energy to fill out the pre-test to the best of their ability or showed up to the session a few minutes too late. That being said, we can still garner significant insight from the score of 9 that was given on the post-test since it represents one of the best post-session answers we have received. This score represents an excellent score for a post-workshop assessment.

It is important to note, however, that these responses gave almost no answers that displayed Capstone level knowledge in our rubric. This is because Faith Zone is only intended to bring participants to a level 2; the higher levels of understanding are what we would expect from more experienced student leadership. To display a capstone response, we have included below two responses to this same question that were written by members of our multifaith advisory council. These responses were given in response to an email prompt I sent them at the conclusion of the year.

Example 1

Religious literacy is the knowledge and understanding of the historical context of religion and its connection to human experience and how it plays a role in the human experience of social justice, cross-cultural communication, and peacemaking. In my work as an RA, I need to

1. Recognize dietary needs of each student to make sure that programs are inclusive.
2. Understand that my residents may be coming from communities of less diversity; I will model acceptance and willingness to learn across those differences.
3. Be able to connect residents to religious or spiritual communities and offer related resources.

Category	Grade	Reason
Knowledge	3	Nearly perfect definition and expression of religion as a concept and its relationship to systems of power throughout history.
Ecumenical Orientation	3	Discusses ways to seek out intercultural experiences and bridge differences.
Self-Awareness and Reflection	3	Discusses the relationship between personal role on campus and personal identity when working with other groups.
Application	3	Gives three correct responses and includes new ideas for solving larger problems.

Example 2

One who is religiously literate is aware and knowledgeable not only of his or her individual spiritual or religious practice or tradition, but also aware, knowledgeable, and respectful of those that others around the world practice. Religious literacy impacts my work because:

1. It reminds me to respect diversity in its many forms and its many faces.
2. It helps me to remain conscious of the environment and people around me, thereby helping me to be respectful and compassionate toward others, especially in difficult situations.
3. It helps me to understand events in the world as more than conflicts between generalized forces/parties/entities.

Category	Grade	Reason
Knowledge	3	Gives a good explanation of religion and later connects religion to greater global systems.
Ecumenical Orientation	3	Discusses respecting diversity and seeking out relationships with others across cultural lines.
Self-Awareness and Reflection	2	Well-articulated relationship between personal role/work and religious diversity, but not an account of personal identity and its impact on this work.
Application	3	Gives three applications and insight into create applications for solving larger global geopolitical issues.

These two examples display how a student leader, after attending a Faith Zone workshop and participating in numerous events run by our office would come to a very high level of religious literacy by the conclusion of his or her time at NYU. This is one of the primary goals of GSL at NYU, and it shows how this rubric effectively measures both Faith Zone sessions and the broader development of students through participation in office programming.

Session Feedback

In addition to direct evaluation questions, we have also received an immense amount of feedback over the past few years about how participants have felt after their experiences in a Faith Zone workshop. Copied below are selected pieces of feedback that we have received on Faith Zone evaluation forms to give a sense of the different ways Faith Zone has impacted participants.

*   I thought this was great, and the balance of conversation/education was perfect. Well done!
*   This training is most helpful because it opens a safe avenue for the campus community. It allows us to explore different religions and enrich

our own faith through our desired beliefs. It helps us in our places of work to become less judgmental of others.

- I was able to talk about my own experiences in a way I did not think about before.
- Co-learner approach—I felt very comfortable speaking and sharing. At other . . . trainings I felt like facilitators were placing themselves above the group. I felt at the same level here.
- Great session! This is such a controversial topic and [the facilitator] did a great job at norm setting and providing useful information. I think of all topics, this is the one least talked about and it is important. I think this is one of the "hidden" issues on campus and hope these sessions continue to happen!
- Establishing, and managing/encouraging the use of "I" statements. The experience also felt judgment free to me. I have attended other [trainings] where I felt there was a "right" and "wrong" response from the facilitators.
- Having an open dialogue with peers from different backgrounds and watching the chaplain video provided me with new knowledge and understanding about what faith means to others.

Moreover, we have also collected testimonials from various Faith Zone trainers themselves to discuss the impact that Faith Zone has had on their campus experience. These responses were given in response to a prompt asking them to evaluate whether Faith Zone is a valuable tool for the NYU community.

- Faith Zone really drove home for me how people arrive at their beliefs or lack of beliefs for perfectly good reasons, and that those reasons tend to come with really interesting and even moving personal stories. Faith Zone seems to help the participant (and myself as facilitator!) put faces and people to views that might otherwise be misunderstood. It also opened my eyes to how religious views and religious presentation can intersect with other aspects of social identity, and how my own and others' spirituality has been influenced by culture(s), sexual orientation, gender(s), education, class, etc. This has resulted in my becoming much more open-minded about others' beliefs—even when wildly differing, and even when those beliefs result in a value system different from mine. I also think that I now make far fewer assumptions about other people's viewpoints based on appearance (due to having been surprised so many times during Faith Zone by being wrong about my assumptions—then catching that I made an unconscious assumption during that moment of surprise). I've learned that people express their spirituality in a way that's personal to them, and fewer outward religious "contradictions" surprise me now. It was an honor to get to present the Faith Zone curriculum because doing so inherently meant getting to attend repeatedly, learning new lessons from participants' answers every time.

—Former NYU Student in the Silver School of Social Work

- Faith Zone is valuable because it presents a strong argument for understanding religious diversity and provides the practical steps towards integrating that understanding into one's work. Through numerous experiences as a student at NYU, I developed a passion for interfaith work and understanding religious difference. Faith Zone gave me the tools, the vocabulary, and the information to be a more effective leader in interreligious and intercultural settings.

—Student President of Bridges; Muslim Jewish
Interfaith Dialogue at NYU

- Working with the NYU Faith Zone program expanded my understanding of and appreciation for diversity at NYU. Through my experiences working with the curriculum and facilitating workshops, I was able to connect with NYU students, faculty, and staff to bring a better understanding of how to create an inclusive campus that promotes dialogue across difference. I have enjoyed bringing what I learned to other professional, personal, and academic experiences, and would strongly suggest participating in Faith Zone and other NYU Global Spiritual Life programs.

—Former NYU Student in the Silver School of Social Work

- Faith Zone encourages the campus community to be intentional and courageous in engaging conversations across difference. Religion does not have to be avoided as a topic in polite company when approached with respect and intentionality. Faith Zone training offers skills and practice at entering and building community through these conversations.

—Christian Chaplain at NYU

- Faith Zone is such an important training to have as part of the "Zone" series because it provides participants with the opportunity to explore and reflect upon their own experiences with religious institutions, faith, and spirituality. The training also helps participants to gain more awareness and knowledge of other religious and spiritual practices. Faith Zone allows us to reflect on how faith and spirituality shows up within NYU and to explore proactive ways we can each work within our own spheres of influence to create a welcoming and inclusive environment for all. Participating in this Zone training has helped to increase my own religious literacy and my awareness of the needs of fellow members of the NYU community. I also participated in the train-the-trainer session as a way to deepen my own understanding of the content presented in the session and also with the goal of being able to share this Zone training with more members of our community.

—Housing Director at NYU

• I believe a curriculum like Faith Zone is important because even people who are well-versed in the skills of exchange across difference experience hesitancy in having conversations with people of different worldviews. It's a messy topic, and the curriculum helps participants wrestle with their own stories in a way that will allow them to open the topic to others too. I think it's also helpful to get a little taste of the research that shows the importance of the conversation as well, because simply knowing that students have expressed wanting space to discuss these topics is important in creating space for discussion to happen.

—Housing Director at NYU

• Faith and spirituality is often not discussed across beliefs in a way that normalizes it. Faith Zone is such a great opportunity for individuals to engage and learn about different faith and religious beliefs regardless of their affiliation. Such great dialogue is important within a university community as our populations continue to become more and more diverse.

—Housing Director at NYU

• In a world rocked by political and social turmoil, it is essential that everyone understand the role that religion plays in people's lives. Faith Zone offers an opportunity for participants to find common ground in their own experiences and to practice open and compassionate communication. Whenever I facilitate a training, I hear people exclaim: "Why isn't this a workshop required for every student, faculty member and administrator?" It is that important.

—Humanist Chaplain at NYU

In summary, through a mix of qualitative and quantitative measures, we can display that Faith Zone has transformed the campus environment at NYU. Not only have we met our initial learning outcomes, but the presence of such a program has expanded our community's notion of diversity education and provided a valuable resource to the university.

Note

1 All data end with the Faith Zone session conducted on October 28, 2016.

7 Bringing Faith Zone to Your Campus

If you are still reading this book after an entire chapter on data and educational outcomes, then there is a considerable chance you want to begin creating a religious literacy program on your campus as quickly as possible. To help translate this workshop to other campuses, I thought it would be helpful to conclude by looking at some of the ways that other campuses will differ from the context and climate at NYU, and discussing the challenges that are most commonly faced by those trying to create religious literacy workshops on college campuses around the country.

There are many types of universities in the United States, but the two that present the starkest contrast with NYU are public universities and religiously affiliated universities. At public universities, discussions about religion and spirituality are often complicated by the legally mandated separation of church and state upon which all federal and state grants are dependent. This often leads schools to avoid any conversation about religion and spirituality to prevent any possible missteps or favoring of one religion at the expense of another. As summarized by Robert Nash in his seminal *Religious Pluralism in the Academy*, "Some educational leaders mistakenly believe that the First Amendment requires a strict separation between Church and state, religion and the academy."[1] This avoidance, however, completely misunderstands the requirements for secular universities to educate students about religion while not promoting any specific religion. As expressed by Associate Justice Tom Clark in Supreme Court decision of Abington Township v. Schempp:

> It might well be said that one's education is not complete without a study of comparative religion or the history of religion and its relationship to the advancement of civilization. It certainly may be said that the Bible is worthy of study for its literary and historic qualities. Nothing we have said here indicates that such study of the Bible or of religion, when presented objectively as part of a secular program of education, may not be effected consistently with the First Amendment.[2]

According to Justice Clark, not only does the First Amendment not prohibit the discussion of religion in the classroom, but an education that does not actually discuss these topics should be considered incomplete. Not only are discussions about religion and spirituality legally permitted at public universities, but there are already examples of public universities in the United States that have begun using Faith Zone. Utah State University partnered with our office to create their own version of Faith Zone, called Better Together Interfaith Allies Training,[3] which has been a staple of their campus since 2013. This program has been incredibly successful and serves as a model for how a public university can incorporate a religious literacy curriculum into their campus programs.

The second type of university whose context differs substantially from NYU is religiously affiliated institutions. These schools present a unique challenge for any religious literacy curriculum because the student bodies are often less religiously diverse than other schools. Despite these differences, however, there are circumstances in which a Faith Zone workshop could be an effective tool at religiously affiliated universities. At a school such as Yeshiva University, whose undergraduate student body is 100 percent Jewish, a workshop that relies so heavily on student experiences to generate discussions about religious diversity might not be the best fit.[4] While there are certainly intragroup conversations that could be conducted, it would require significant modifications to the Faith Zone curriculum and would effectively be a different workshop altogether. On the other hand, at a university like Notre Dame whose incoming first-year student body was 80 percent Catholic,[5] a workshop such as Faith Zone would be entirely possible as long as the room itself was made diverse. There is no reason why a workshop that is made up of mostly Catholic participants could still not engage in serious conversations bout religious diversity, assuming the workshop were run by experienced and skilled facilitators who knew how to discuss the diversity in the room without tokenizing members of smaller religious groups. An excellent example of this type of work is the Center for the Study of Jewish–Christian–Muslim Relations[6] at Merrimack University (a Catholic university in Massachusetts), which brought me in for a Faith Zone workshop in the Fall of 2015 and has piloted numerous fantastic interfaith programs. Therefore, even though religious literacy workshops at more religiously homogeneous schools can be more complicated than at secular universities, there are enough examples of successful programs to suggest that these workshops can be run effectively, no matter the campus.

Besides these structural issues, there are also challenges that can arise at any university when introducing conversations about religious and spiritual diversity for the first time. I will focus on three main challenges in this chapter that occur most regularly on campuses around the world, and explain how we have handled them at NYU.

The first challenge is how to approach issues of representation and equity as they relate to the various religious groups on campus. Different religious communities will have access to vastly different levels of funding, off-campus communal support, and on-campus chaplain availability, all of which contribute to varying levels of organizational and programmatic confidence among students. For example, Catholic,[7] Jewish,[8] and Protestant[9] students all have a variety of national organizations with placements at campuses across the country providing resources for students and enabling groups to grow and sustain larger communities. In contrast, there is no national sending agency for Buddhist, Muslim, or Sikh chaplains, and the lack of official ordination makes finding and appointing Sikh chaplains at various campuses extremely difficult. These representational challenges, coupled with the demographics of religious groups in the United States, make developing fully equitable representation of different religions extremely difficult at any center focused on religious and spiritual life. Without this representation, it can be difficult to construct a religious literacy program that is fully responsive to everyone, especially groups that are already marginalized. To deal with this challenge, special care and consideration need to go into cultivating student leadership and community resources for marginalized groups before creating any religious literacy programs. By incorporating people from these groups at the outset, it is more likely that these challenges can be met and your religious literacy program can be more fully inclusive.

The second challenge to creating these programs is the impact of direct geopolitical conflicts on the relationships between student groups. College campuses have long been a hotbed for political activism in the United States, and our current campus climate is no different. Most of these issues do not directly fall along religious lines, but issues such as the Israeli–Palestinian conflict can sometimes drive a wedge between specific religious groups. Whether or not this topic should be a part of Muslim–Jewish dialogue is vigorously debated among interfaith advocates and political organizers alike, but there are examples from across the country of this topic becoming a source of tension for students within multifaith settings.[10] Unfortunately, this book is not the proper avenue to fully articulate various solutions to this challenge, but recognizing the conflict's impact on campus communities and being aware of its potential to create conflict is critical when establishing religious literacy programs.

The third and final challenge to teaching this material is that the skill set necessary for facilitating and creating workshops is not always similar to the skill set needed to evaluate their success. At NYU, we have spent countless hours consulting with the Office of Research and Assessment trying to develop our assessment tools and abilities. We are fortunate to have this resource, but similar resources are not available everywhere and present a serious challenge for schools trying to create their own programs. For this reason, we have tried to incorporate everything we use for program assessment at NYU into this book so that campuses with fewer resources can replicate our assessment as much as possible. Ultimately, however, religious literacy programs are only as strong as their assessment, and the field will be unable to grow without sustained and rigorous assessment of our programs.

Into the Future

As universities across the world begin to engineer more intentional conversations about religious and spiritual diversity, tools to effectively facilitate these conversations are going to become increasingly important. At NYU, we receive multiple calls each week from other universities around the world asking for details and advice about how to create centers for religious and spiritual life on their campus, and how to create educational materials to teach religious literacy to the community at large. This book has focused on the approach we use at NYU, and we hope that many elements of this approach will be applicable to your campus.

Since the founding of our office 4 years ago, there has already been substantial expansion of religious literacy programs across various institutions in the United States. Dr. Marcella Runell Hall, creator of the original religious literacy curriculum at NYU, is now the Vice President of Student Life at Mount Holyoke College and has brought components of this program with her to their campus. Additionally, in her time at NYU, Dr. Hall collaborated with Utah State University and helped them create their own religious literacy curriculum, which they have been using on campus for the last 2 years. More recently, I have conducted religious literacy trainings for Lafayette College, Merrimack College, The Pennsylvania Consortium for the Liberal Arts, and Lehigh University, and I have also had contact with a minimum of 15 other universities in the United States to advise them as they begin the process of developing their own curricula. None of these programs existed even 5 years ago, and more will continue to develop as religious literacy curricula become more easily accessible and available throughout higher education.

Ultimately, religious literacy will continue to become a more central element of diversity education at universities across the country, and our approach to answering these questions will, in part, determine the success of our education system moving forward. Research continuously shows us that our students are concerned with religious and spiritual questions, and that they are extremely diverse, as well as religiously illiterate. Will we respond to this dynamic by making religious literacy central to education, or will we allow our students to graduate unable to display a nuanced and complex sense of religious literacy? The Office of Global Spiritual Life at NYU is committed "to educating and inspiring religious and spiritual leaders to utilize multifaith dialogue and service as a force for positive social change," and we hope that the system of higher education in the United States will join us in this mission.

Notes

1 Nash, *Religious Pluralism*, 5.
2 Moore, "Overcoming Religious Illiteracy."
3 "Better Together Interfaith Allies Training," *Utah State University*, accessed November 1, 2016, https://interfaith.usu.edu/getinvolved/oncampus/bettertogether.
4 "2015 Top 60 Schools by Jewish Student Population," *News and Views—Blog*, accessed June 24, 2015, http://www.hillel.org/about/news-views/news-views-blog/news-and-views/2015/06/24/2015-top-60-schools-by-jewish-student-population.
5 "Admission Statistics // Undergraduate Admissions // University of Notre Dame." *Undergraduate Admissions*, accessed November 1, 2016, http://admissions.nd.edu/apply/admission-statistics/.
6 "Center for the Study of Jewish-Christian-Muslim-Relations," *Merrimack College*, accessed November 1, 2016, https://www.merrimack.edu/academics/centers/jcmr/.
7 Such as FOCUS Ministries and Newman Centers.
8 Such as Hillel, Chabbad, and Meor.
9 Such as Campus Crusade for Christ, Intervarsity Christian Fellowship, and Canterbury Episcopal Campus Ministries.
10 Linda K. Wertheimer, "Students and the Middle East Conflict," *The New York Times*, August 7, 2016, http://www.nytimes.com/2016/08/07/education/edlife/middle-east-conflict-on-campus-anti-semitism.html.

Appendix A

University	LGBTQ	Multicultural	Spiritual Life
Princeton	2	2	2
Harvard	2	1	1
Yale	2	1	2
Columbia	2	2	1
Stanford	2	1	2
University of Chicago	2	2	2
MIT	2	2	1
Duke	2	2	1
University of Pennsylvania	2	2	1
California Institute of Technology	1	1	0
Johns Hopkins	2	2	2
Dartmouth	1	2	2
Northwestern	1	2	2
Brown	2	2	2
Cornell	2	2	2
Vanderbilt	1	2	2
Washington University in St. Louis	0	2	0
Rice University	1	2	1
UC Berkeley	2	2	0
Emory	2	2	2
Carnegie Mellon	2	0	0
UCLA	2	1	0
University of Southern California	2	0	2
University of Virginia	1	2	0
Tufts	2	1	2

(*Continued*)

(Continued)

University	LGBTQ	Multicultural	Spiritual Life
Wake Forest	2	2	1
University of Michigan Ann Arbor	2	2	1
UNC Chapel Hill	2	1	0
NYU	2	2	2
University of Rochester	2	2	2
Brandeis	2	2	1
University of William and Mary	1	2	0
Georgia Institute of Technology	2	0	0
Case Western Reserve	2	2	0
UC Santa Barbara	2	2	0
UC Irvine	2	2	0
UC San Diego	2	2	1
Boston University	0	1	1
Rensselaer Polytechnic Institute	0	0	1
Tulane University	2	2	0
UC Davis	2	2	0
University of Illinois Urbana-Champaign	2	1	0
University of Wisconsin Madison	2	2	0
Lehigh University	2	2	1
Northeastern University	2	2	2
Penn State University Park	2	2	2
University of Florida	2	2	1
University of Miami	2	2	1
The Ohio State University, Columbus	0	2	0
UT Austin	2	2	0
U of Washington	2	2	0
George Washington University	2	2	0
U of Connecticut	2	0	0
U of Maryland College Park	2	2	1
Worcester Polytechnic Institute	0	2	2
Clemson U	1	1	0
Purdue U, West Lafayette	2	1	0
Syracuse	2	2	1
U of Georgia	2	2	0
U of Pittsburgh	1	2	1
U of Minnesota Twin Cities	2	2	0

University	LGBTQ	Multicultural	Spiritual Life
Texas A&M College Station	2	1	1
Virginia Tech	0	2	0
American U	0	2	2
Rutgers, New Brunswick	2	2	0
Clark	0	1	0
Colorado School of Mines	0	1	0
Indiana U—Bloomington	2	1	0
Michigan State U	2	2	0
Stevens Institute of Tech	0	0	0
U of Delaware	2	0	1
UMass Amherst	2	2	2
Miami U Oxford	1	1	0
UC Santa Cruz	2	0	0
U of Iowa	2	2	0
U of Denver	1	2	2
U of Tulsa	0	2	0
Binghamton U SUNY	0	2	0
North Carolina State U Raleigh	2	2	0
Stony Brook SUNY	2	2	2
SUNY College of Environmental Science and Forestry	0	0	0
CU Boulder	2	2	0
U of Vermont	2	2	1
Florida State	2	1	1
U of Alabama	0	1	1
Drexel U	1	2	1
U of Buffalo SUNY	1	2	2
Auburn U	0	2	0
U of Missouri	2	2	0
U of Nebraska Lincoln	2	2	0
U of New Hampshire	0	2	1
U of Oregon	2	2	0
U of Tennessee	2	2	1
Illinois Institute of Tech	1	1	0
Iowa State	2	2	0

(*Continued*)

(Continued)

University	LGBTQ	Multicultural	Spiritual Life
U of Oklahoma	2	2	0
U of South Carolina	0	2	0
U of the Pacific	2	2	2
University of Utah	2	2	0

Appendix B

	Variable Name	Survey Question/Explanation	Code-Possible Values
D	school	[Add schools to Code Book as they come in]	
E	position	Role on Campus	1,0,2 (staff, student, guest)
F	netid	NYU only	Write in
G	t1religlitA	Please define religious literacy and describe three concrete ways it impacts your work. Definition of Religious Literacy.	0–3 (scale)
H	t1religlitB	Please define religious literacy and describe three concrete ways it impacts your work. Application of Religious Literacy.	0–3 (scale)
I	t1religlitC	Please define religious literacy and describe three concrete ways it impacts your work. Identity and Self-Awareness.	0–3 (scale)
J	t1religlitD	Please define religious literacy and describe three concrete ways it impacts your work. Diversity of Faiths and Cultures.	0–3 (scale)
K	t1religlittotal (0–12)	Please define religious literacy and describe three concrete ways it impacts your work.	0–12 (scale)
L	t1religlitfulltext	Please define religious literacy and describe three concrete ways it impacts your work.	Write in

(*Continued*)

(Continued)

	Variable Name	Survey Question/Explanation	Code-Possible Values
M	t2religlitA	Please define religious literacy and describe three concrete ways it impacts your work. Definition of Religious Literacy.	0–3 (scale)
N	t2religlitB	Please define religious literacy and describe three concrete ways it impacts your work. Application of Religious Literacy.	0–3 (scale)
O	t2religlitC	Please define religious literacy and describe three concrete ways it impacts your work. Identity and Self-Awareness.	0–3 (scale)
P	t2religlitD	Please define religious literacy and describe three concrete ways it impacts your work. Diversity of Faiths and Cultures.	0–3 (scale)
Q	t2religlittotal (0–12)	Please define religious literacy and describe three concrete ways it impacts your work.	0–12 (scale)
R	t2religlitfulltext	Please define religious literacy and describe three concrete ways it impacts your work.	Write in
S	changereliglittotal	Please define religious literacy and describe three concrete ways it impacts your work.	Automatic Equation
T	t1programs	Please list three programs that are available through Global Spiritual Life at NYU.	1–3 (# of correct)
U	t1programsfulltext	Please list three programs that are available through Global Spiritual Life at NYU.	Write In
V	t2programs	Please list three programs that are available through Global Spiritual Life at NYU.	1–3 (# of correct)
W	t2programsfulltext	Please list three programs that are available through Global Spiritual Life at NYU.	Write In

	Variable Name	Survey Question/Explanation	Code-Possible Values
X	t1centers	Please list three centers and/ or groups of religious life on campus.	1–3 (# of correct)
Y	t1centersfulltext	Please list three centers and/ or groups of religious life on campus.	Write In
Z	t2centers	Please list three centers and/ or groups of religious life on campus.	1–3 (# of correct)
AA	t2centersfulltext	Please list three centers and/ or groups of religious life on campus.	Write In
AB	foundationknow	Faith Zone provided a foundation of knowledge needed the facilitate effective dialogue around spiritual issues and concerns.	1–5 (scale)
AC	foundationle	What was most effective?	Write in
AD	foundationme	What was least effective?	Write in
AE	usefultools	Faith Zone provided useful tools and information to create a safe and comfortable environment in my interactions across different NYU spaces	1–5 (scale)
AF	usefultoolsme	What was most effective?	Write in
AG	usefultoolsle	What was least effective?	Write in
AH	safeenviron	Faith Zone provided a safe environment for useful, structured dialogue and learning around religious and spiritual identities.	1–5 (scale)
AI	safeenvironme	What was most effective?	Write in
AJ	safeenvironle	What was least effective?	Write in
AK	comments	Please provide any additional feedback or comments? How can GSL improve this training?	Write In

(Continued)

(Continued)

	Variable Name	Survey Question/Explanation	Code-Possible Values
AL	Race	Race (check all that apply):	1 = African/ African, American/ Black, 2 = Arab/ Arab American, 3 = Asian/Asian American/ Pacific Islander, 4 = Biracial/ Multiracial (accompanied by write in), 5 = Latino/a, 6 = Native American/ American Indian/ Indigenous, 7 = White/ European American, 8 = Other (accompanied by write in)
AM	Gender	Gender (check all that apply):	1 = Woman, 2 = Man, 3 = Transgender, 4 = Cisgender, 5 = Gender nonconforming/ Genderqueer, 6 = Option not listed (accompanied by write in), 7 = Prefer not to answer
AN	Sexual Orientation	Sexual Orientation (check all that apply):	1 = Lesbian, 2 = Gay, 3 = Bisexual/ Pansexual, 4 = Straight, 5 = Queer, 6 = Asexual, 7 = Option not listed (accompanied by write in), 8 = Prefer not to answer

	Variable Name	Survey Question/Explanation	Code-Possible Values
AO	Religious Affiliation	Religious Affiliation (check all that apply):	1 = Catholic, 2 = Protestant, 3 = Muslim, 4 = Jewish, 5 = Atheist, 6 = Agnostic, 7 = Buddhist, 8 = Hindu, 9 = Humanist, 10 = Prefer not to answer, 11 = Spiritual but not religious, 12 = Other (accompanied by write in) 666—Blank Response

Appendix C

Religion	Spirituality
Rituals	Individual
Institutions	Personal
Prayer	Mindfulness
God	Yoga
Laws	Mediation
Oppression	Inspiration
War	Oneness
Sexism	Interconnectedness
Inspiration	Don't need God
Revelation	Vague
Holidays	Hippies
Family	Naval gazing
Government	Emotions
Politics	Practice
Organizations	Earth and nature
Food	Identity
Culture	Humanity
History	Hope
Diversity	Beliefs
Sexism	Divinity

References

"2015 Top 60 Schools by Jewish Student Population." News and Views—Blog. Accessed June 24, 2015. http://www.hillel.org/about/news-views/news-views-blog/news-and-views/2015/06/24/2015-top-60-schools-by-jewish-student-population.

"Action Zone Bystander Intervention." New York University. http://www.nyu.edu/students/health-and-wellness/student-health-center/programs-events/action-zone.html.

Adams, Maurianne, Lee Anne Bell, and Pat Griffin. *Teaching for Diversity and Social Justice: A Sourcebook*. New York, NY: Routledge, 1997.

"Admission Statistics // Undergraduate Admissions // University of Notre Dame." Undergraduate Admissions. Accessed November 1, 2016. http://admissions.nd.edu/apply/admission-statistics/.

Astin, Alexander W., Helen S. Astin, and Jennifer A. Lindholm. "Assessing Students' Spiritual and Religious Qualities." *Journal of College Student Development* 52, no. 1 (2011): 39–61. doi:10.1353/csd.2011.0009.

Astin, Alexander W., Helen S. Astin, and Jennifer A. Lindholm. *Cultivating the Spirit: How College Can Enhance Students' Inner Lives*. San Francisco: Jossey-Bass, 2011.

"The Best Colleges in America, Ranked." U.S. News and World Report. 2015. http://colleges.usnews.rankingsandreviews.com/best-colleges.

"Better Together Interfaith Allies Training." Utah State University. Accessed November 1, 2016. https://interfaith.usu.edu/getinvolved/oncampus/bettertogether.

"Center for the Study of Jewish-Christian-Muslim-Relations." Merrimack College. Accessed November 1, 2016. https://www.merrimack.edu/academics/centers/jcmr/.

"Curricula for Educators." Tanenbaum Center for Religious Understanding. Accessed March 30, 2016. https://tanenbaum.org/ https://tanenbaum.org/product-category/curricula/.

"Directory of Religious Centers." The Pluralism Project at Harvard University. Accessed March 30, 2016. http://www.pluralism.org/interfaith/directory.

"Eboo Patel on the Future of Multifaith." In *Multifaithful Podcast*. December 2, 2015.

Eck, Diana. "What Is Pluralism." The Pluralism Project at Harvard University. 2006. http://pluralism.org/what-is-pluralism/.

"Focus Areas for Student Affairs Professionals." NASPA. Accessed March 30, 2016. https://www.naspa.org/focus-areas.

Ganz, Marshall. "Telling Your Public Story: Self, Us, Now." 2007. https://philstesthomepage.files.wordpress.com/2014/05/public-story-worksheet07ganz.pdf.

"God, Baseball and the Spirit of NYU (Part 1)." In *Multifaithful Podcast*. November 18, 2015.

"Guidelines for Discussing Difficult or Controversial Topics." Center for Research on Learning and Teaching. Accessed November 1, 2016. http://www.crlt.umich.edu/publinks/generalguidelines.

"Guidelines for Healthy Dialogue." Free Minds Free People. Accessed November 1, 2016. https://fmfp.org/about/guidelines-for-healthy-dialogue/.

"Guidelines for Interfaith Dialogue." Religion Communicators Council. Accessed November 1, 2016. http://www.religioncommunicators.org/guidelines-for-interfaith-dialogue.

Heckman, Bud. "Religious Literacy." Religion Communicators Council. Accessed March 30, 2016. http://www.religioncommunicators.org/religious-literacy.

hooks, bell. *Teaching Community: A Pedagogy of Hope*. New York: Routledge, 2003.

Jacobsen, Douglas G. and Rhonda Hustedt Jacobsen. *No Longer Invisible: Religion in University Education*. Oxford: Oxford University Press, 2012.

Jones, Robert. "Religious Affiliation of New York Residents by Borough—PRRI." PRRI. Accessed September 22, 2015. http://www.prri.org/spotlight/religious-affiliation-of-new-york-residents-by-borough/.

Lindholm, Jennifer A. *A Guidebook of Promising Practices: Facilitating College Students' Spiritual Development*. Oakland: Regents of the University of California, 2011.

Liu, Joseph. "The Global Religious Landscape." Pew Research Centers Religion Public Life Project RSS. Accessed December 18, 2012. http://www.pewforum.org/2012/12/18/global-religious-landscape-exec/.

Luria, Isaac. "Why We're Building an Ark." Sojourners. Accessed May 6, 2015. https://sojo.net/articles/why-we-re-building-ark.

"Meet the Board—Seeds of Peace." Seeds of Peace. Accessed March 30, 2016. http://www.seedsofpeace.org/board/.

Moore, Diane L. "Overcoming Religious Illiteracy: A Cultural Studies Approach." *World History Connected* 4, no. 1. Diane L. Moore: Overcoming Religious Illiteracy: A Cultural Studies Approach. November 2006. http://worldhistoryconnected.press.illinois.edu/4.1/moore.html.

Moore, Diane L. *Overcoming Religious Illiteracy: A Cultural Studies Approach to the Study of Religion in Secondary Education*. New York: Palgrave Macmillan, 2007.

Moore, Diane L. "Definition of Religious Literacy." Religious Literacy Project. Accessed February 23, 2016. http://rlp.hds.harvard.edu/definition-religious-literacy.

Nash, Robert J. *Religious Pluralism in the Academy: Opening the Dialogue*. New York: P. Lang, 2001.

"NYU Ally Week." NYU Ally Week. Accessed February 23, 2016. https://www.nyu.edu/life/events-traditions/nyu-ally-week.html.

"Of Many Institute." Of Many Institute at NYU. Accessed November 1, 2016. https://www.nyu.edu/students/communities-and-groups/student-diversity/spiritual-life/of-many-institute-for-multifaith-leadership.html.

Patel, Eboo. "Eboo Patel: Look to Young People for Leadership in Interfaith Cooperation." Faith and Leadership. Accessed October 10, 2011. https://www.faithandleadership.com/qa/eboo-patel-look-young-people-for-leadership-interfaith-cooperation.

Patel, Eboo. "In Promoting Campus Diversity, Don't Dismiss Religion." The Chronicle of Higher Education. Accessed March 11, 2015. http://chronicle.com/article/In-Promoting-Campus-Diversity/228427/.

Peace Players International. Accessed March 30, 2016. https://www.peaceplayersintl.org/.

Prothero, Stephen R. *Religious Literacy: What Every American Needs to Know*. San Francisco, CA: Harper San Francisco, 2007.

Redden, Elizabeth. "Global Ambitions." Inside Higher Education. Accessed March 11, 2013. https://www.insidehighered.com/news/2013/03/11/nyu-establishes-campuses-and-sites-around-globe.

"Religion." Merriam-Webster. http://www.merriam-webster.com/dictionary/religion?utm_campaign=sd&utm_medium=serp&utm_source=jsonld.

"Religion." Oxford Dictionaries. https://en.oxforddictionaries.com/definition/religion.

"Religions Are Internally Diverse." Harvard Divinity School Religious Literacy Project. Accessed March 30, 2016. http://rlp.hds.harvard.edu/religions-are-internally-diverse.

"Religious Affiliation of New York Residents by Borough." PRRI. Accessed September 22, 2015. http://www.prri.org/spotlight/religious-affiliation-of-new-york-residents-by-borough/.

Rockenbach, Alyssa Bryant and Matthew J. Mayhew. "How the Collegiate Religious and Spiritual Climate Shapes Students' Ecumenical Orientation." *Research in Higher Education* 54, no. 4 (2013): 461–479. doi:10.1007/s11162-013-9282-y.

"SafeZone: NYU's Ally Program." New York University. http://www.nyu.edu/students/communities-and-groups/student-diversity/lesbian-gay-bisexual-transgender-and-queer-student-center/education-advocacy-and-trainings/safezone.html.

"Spirituality." Merriam-Webster. http://www.merriam-webster.com/dictionary/spirituality.

"Spirituality." Oxford Dictionaries. https://en.oxforddictionaries.com/definition/spiritual.

"Spirituality and Religion in Higher Education | NASPA." NASPA. Accessed March 30, 2016. https://www.naspa.org/constituent-groups/kcs/spirituality-and-religion-in-higher-education.

Tisdell, Elizabeth. *Exploring Spirituality and Culture in Adult and Higher Education*. San Francisco: Jossey-Bass, 2003.

Tisdell, Elizabeth. "The Connection of Spirituality to Culturally Responsive Teaching in Higher Education." *Spirituality in Higher Education* 1, no. 4 (2004): 1–9. http://spirituality.ucla.edu/docs/newsletters/1/Tisdell.pdf.

"VALUE Rubrics." Association of American Colleges & Universities. Accessed June 26, 2015. https://www.aacu.org/value-rubrics.

Wertheimer, Linda K. "Students and the Middle East Conflict." *The New York Times*, August 7, 2016. http://www.nytimes.com/2016/08/07/education/edlife/middle-east-conflict-on-campus-anti-semitism.html.

"World Religions Through Their Scriptures." EdX. Accessed March 21, 2016. https://www.edx.org/xseries/world-religions-through-scriptures.

Wormald, Benjamin. "Religious Landscape Study." Pew Research Centers Religion Public Life Project RSS. Accessed May 11, 2015. http://www.pewforum.org/religious-landscape-study/.

Zacharias, Ravi. "Defending Christianity in a Secular Culture." RZIM. Accessed January 26, 2009. http://rzim.org/just-thinking/defending-christianity-in-a-secular-culture.

"Zone Trainings." New York University. https://www.nyu.edu/students/communities-and-groups/student-diversity/multicultural-education-and-programs/what-we-do/social-justice-education/zone-trainings.html.

Index

For Product Safety Concerns and Information please contact our EU representative GPSR@taylorandfrancis.com Taylor & Francis Verlag GmbH, Kaufingerstraße 24, 80331 München, Germany

Printed and bound by CPI Group (UK) Ltd, Croydon, CR0 4YY

11/04/2025

01844010-0003